# THE SYLLABUS / E-SYLLABUS FOR THE 21ST CENTURY

**Jack Gifford**

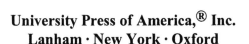

**University Press of America,® Inc.**
Lanham · New York · Oxford

Copyright © 2003 by
University Press of America,® Inc.
4501 Forbes Boulevard, Suite 200
Lanham, Maryland 20706

PO Box 317
Oxford
OX2 9RU, UK

ISBN 0-7618-2499-5 (paperback : alk. ppr.)

# Contents

Preface

# Figures

# Preface

Having taught for over thirty years at Miami University (Ohio) and the University of Colorado, I have been constantly amazed by what most of my colleagues refer to as their syllabi. I have also reviewed over 100 e-syllabi, plus dozens of syllabi used by my colleagues throughout the United States, UK and Western Europe. At worst the syllabus doesn't exist. Only slightly better is a schedule of classroom activities and assigned chapters. Nowhere are the students informed about the reason for taking the course, the philosophy behind its pedagogy and content, the hopes and dreams of their teacher, and the rules by which their behavior and learning will be assessed. The great majority of teachers in high schools, colleges and universities still print out their syllabus for distribution on the first day of class. This assumes that they know what the needs of the students will be for the next several months, and that they can predict how this should be structured and communicated. Teaching a course from semester to semester may involve little more than changing the dates on the schedule of activities.

With the arrival of personal computers, the Internet, easy web construction packages, and the potential for communicating with your students 24/7 outside of the classroom, we have been given the opportunity to enrich our lives and those of our students through the creation of a living and dynamic web page e-syllabus. We can change and add materials as they become available. Students can work in electronic teams and access information resources, both documents and humans, from around the world. Pre- and post-class discussions are possible to enrich almost any topic. The possibilities are endless.

To develop a well organized and educationally sound e-syllabus, a number of mental steps must occur before the first word is entered on your e-syllabus. In this book I have attempted to provide a concise and complete guide these preparatory mental activities, followed by a structured set of guidelines for the actual creation of an e-syllabus. Also included is a check sheet against which you can assess the contents of your own e-syllabus. The final major section of this book contains an actual e-syllabus used by the author that contains 95% of everything discussed in the book. While we all teach different subjects to students or employees, most of the fundamental structural elements are extremely similar.

Almost no one will use every aspect of an e-syllabus in this book. You should pick and choose those that are appropriate for you, your students, and your particular educational mission. I encourage you to enter this journey with an open mind...and dare to be different. Both you and your students will be the winners. Good luck.

Jack Gifford, Professor of Marketing
Miami Univerisity (Ohio)
Web site: www.ba.muohio.edu/gifforjb.edu/index.htm
Email: gifforjb@muohio.edu

# The Syllabus/E-Syllabus for the 21st Century

*Before you write the first word of your e-syllabus…*

## INTRODUCTION

As a new or experienced teacher, you have seen or created hundreds of syllabi. They were present in almost every one of your high school, community college, undergraduate and graduate classes. If you have been a teacher in any educational institution or training facility, either part time or full time, you have prepared dozens of syllabi. Many of you have incorporated courseware or multi media by placing your syllabi on corporate or school servers, or your own personal web pages. After teaching for over thirty years, seeing and preparing over 75 syllabi in both corporate training centers and higher education, plus reviewing another 120 syllabi, the author has yet to find, or create, the "100% syllabus". All are missing key dimensions, don't reflect internally consistent pre-planning, and most are not presented in a user-friendly manner. We can all do better!

The purpose of this book is to encourage a professional approach to, and development of syllabi, particularly those supported by electronic media. Those e-syllabi that contain any type of materials or information that can be reached beyond the classroom are, by definition, a form of distance learning. In the majority of cases, this can be referred to as "near distance learning" as the audience attends a physical classroom on a regular schedule, but also has access to electronic information in a time and place beyond that classroom.

Figure 1 graphically presents an overview of the content of this book. We will start with an introduction that discusses topics such as: the definition, history and meaning of e-syllabus; why is an e-syllabus

## FIGURE 1: PREPARING AN E-SYLLABUS:

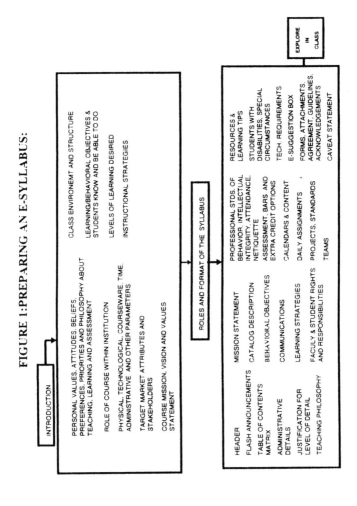

INTRODUCTION

PERSONAL VALUES, ATTITUDES, BELIEFS,
PREFERENCES, PRIORITIES AND PHILOSOPHY ABOUT
TEACHING, LEARNING AND ASSESSMENT

ROLE OF COURSE WITHIN INSTITUTION

PHYSICAL, TECHNOLOGICAL, COURSEWARE, TIME,
ADMINISTRATIVE AND OTHER PARAMETERS

TARGET MARKET ATTRIBUTES AND
STAKEHOLDERS

COURSE MISSION, VISION AND VALUES
STATEMENT

CLASS ENVIRONEMT AND STRUCTURE

LEARNING/BEHAVIORAL OBJECTIVES &
STUDENTS KNOW AND BE ABLE TO DO

LEVELS OF LEARNING DESIRED

INSTRUCTIONAL STRATEGIES

ROLES AND FORMAT OF THE SYLLABUS

HEADER
FLASH ANNOUNCEMENTS
TABLE OF CONTENTS
MATRIX
ADMINISTRATIVE
DETAILS
JUSTIFICATION FOR
LEVEL OF DETAIL
TEACHING PHILOSOPHY

MISSION STATEMENT
CATALOG DESCRIPTION

BEHAVIORAL OBJECTIVES

COMMUNICATIONS

LEARNING STRATEGIES
FACULY & STUDENT RIGHTS
AND RESPONSIBILITIES

PROFESSIONAL STDS. OF
BEHAVIOR, INTELLECTUAL
INTEGRITY, ATTENDANCE,
NETIQUETTE
ASSESSMENT, BARS AND
EXTRA CREDIT OPTIONS

CALENDARS & CONTENT

DAILY ASSIGNMENTS

PROJECTS, STANDARDS

TEAMS

RESOURCES &
LEARNING TIPS
STUDENTS WITH
DISABLITIES, SPECIAL
CIRCUMSTANCES
TECH. REQUIREMENTS
E-SUGGESTION BOX
FORMS, ATTACHMENTS,
AGREEMENT, GUIDELINES,
ACKNOWLEDGEMENTS
CAVEAT STATEMENT

EXPLORE
IN
CLASS

such a big deal; dynamic and multi- dimensional media; benefits to the teacher; benefits to our students, IT and near distance learning in the classroom; the syllabus as a communications medium, legal and copyright issues, the e-syllabus as it relates to the teaching portfolio, assessment and accountability, and the course manual concept.

After this introduction we will jointly explore the nine major steps essential to the conceptual development of any e-syllabus prior to creating the first word of your actual e-syllabus. These steps are absolutely essential for the professional educator to carefully and consciously execute every time they are to teach a course. Only after the completion of these steps can you decide on the roles and format of the e-syllabus, followed by the actual creation of the e-syllabus.

**What is a syllabus and how long have they been around?**

A syllabus is the outcome of curriculum development and contains both an instructional plan and details of the instructional process to be used within a defined unit of study. These units of study could be a corporate training program on leadership, a high school course on American History, or a college or university course in Otorhinolaryngology (head/neck surgery) or the Origins of Western Physical Sciences. They may take written, graphical or electronic form and are often supplement with verbal commentary by the teacher. They represent guidelines for the reader and teacher about a topic or skill to be studied over a defined period of time. The place in which the learning will take place could be a high school classroom, corporate training center, college or university campus, or literally multiple locations across a nation or the globe.

A syllabus is normally prepared by one or more teachers/trainers, although in student-centered learning environments, students take an active role in formulating the syllabus. Most syllabi are both macro and micro in nature with the intent to accomplish defined behavioral objectives through the execution of a series of learning units.

The concept of the syllabus has existed since the beginning of communal mankind. Early hieroglyphics tell stories or lessons organized around people, places and subjects to be communicated to generations that followed. Cicero, in his Genres of Rhetoric or "panegyric and epidictic" in Greek, was a form of syllabus for instruction from a great teacher to learners on virtue, invention, utility, necessity and affection. Plato's seven Tetralogies represent another early "syllabus" formulated into 28 "lesson units" to his students concerning cause, desires, nature, will, judgment, reason and order.

# 4    The Syllabus / E-Syllabus for the 21st Century

Within all the great religions of the worlds we see written documents by great deities or teaches to their followers/students. Almost all these divine works (Koran, Bible, Torah, etc.) are structured around behavioral objectives for followers to know, understand and follow. Each is divided into micro sections within a macro model of beliefs and behavior.

From these early days we can jump to more modern times. In the early nineteenth century, great educators such as Franklin Babbitt, Ralph Tyler, Johann Herbart, and Herbert Spencer wrote many essays and books with titles such as *How to Make a Curriculum, Basic Principles of Curriculum and Instruction: Syllabus for Education, The Science of Education, and Education: Intellectual, Moral and Physical.* In the United States, one of the most significant works, *The Blue Book* (1905) by the United States Board of Education, laid the foundations for the curriculum and methods of teaching based upon a clear determination of the goals, followed by detailed instructional plans and units (syllabi).

It is not the author's intent to provide a history lesson on the historical foundations of the syllabus. Hopefully it is clear to the reader that the concept of the syllabus has existed throughout the recorded history of mankind, has played a vital role throughout all societies, and will continue to play an enormously important role in the 21$^{st}$ century.

**What is a near distance learning e-syllabus?**

According to the American Heritage Dictionary of the English Language (Copyright 2000, Houghton Mifflin Company), syllabus is a noun; an outline or a summary of the main points of a text, lecture or course of study. In law, a syllabus is a short statement preceding a report on an adjudged case and containing a summary of the court's rulings on each point involved. The Cambridge International Dictionary of English (Copyright 2000, Cambridge University Press) defines a syllabus as a plan showing the subjects or books to be studied in a particular course, especially a course which leads to an examination. Its etymology indicates that the word is derived from Medieval Latin, *sillybus*, to put together, and the Greek *sillubos*, parchment label. Near distance learning refers to learning opportunities in a place and time outside of the classroom. The "e" in syllabus refers to the medium in which the syllabus is created and made available to students and other relevant stakeholders. Therefore, the term "near distance e-syllabus" refers to electronically transmitted outlines or summaries of main points within a particular course at a time and place outside the Figure 1 traditional classroom, often resulting in examinations of acquired knowledge and skills.

## Why is a near distance learning e-syllabus such a big deal?

"Whether it is intended or not, the quality of the course outline is a fairly reliable indicator of the quality of teaching and learning that will take place over the course of a semester." (Harriet W. Sheridan Center for Teaching and Learning/Michael Woolcock) "What students accomplish (or fail to accomplish) over the course of the semester, no matter what the subject matter, is a product not only of individual efforts and abilities on the part of students and instructor, but of the very structure of the course itself" [as outlined in the course syllabus]." (Harriet W. Sheridan Center for Teaching and Learning/Michael Woolcock)

The e-syllabus is a big deal! It reflects the quality of thinking of the teacher prior to the creation of the electronic document and facilitates the meeting of well-developed behavioral objectives. It should respond to the learning needs of the students and relevant stakeholders, the role of the course within the curriculum, and the values, attitudes and beliefs of the teacher. It is the dynamic, interactive electronic medium that lays out for the students and others what they will learn, why it is important that this learning takes place, how the knowledge and skills fits with what has proceeded and what will follow, how this knowledge will be acquired, and the means of measuring their level of attainment to be used. As part of your teaching portfolio, it is the foundation upon which your teaching professionalism and accountability will be judged.

According to L. S. Garavalia (Garavalia, L. S. 1999) a syllabus is a big deal because it:

1. Sets the stage for the course;
2. Establishes an early point of contact and connection between student and instructor;
3. Helps set the tone and expectations for your course;
4. Describes your beliefs about the educational purposes;
5. Acquaints students with the logistics of the course
6. Contains collected handouts;
7. Defines students responsibilities for successful course work;
8. Helps students to assess their readiness for your course;
9. Provides a conceptual framework;
10. Describes available resources;
11. Communicates the role of technology in the course;

12. Can improve the effectiveness of student note taking;
13. Can serve as a learning contract;
14. Outlines desired outcomes;
15. Provides parameters within which the course is constructed;
16. Functions as a map for the students;
17. Becomes the basis for a teaching portfolio;
18. Avoids or reduces student-faculty misunderstandings;
19. Serves as semi-binding contractual agreement;
20. Operates as a Communications device;
21. Is part of being a professional educator;
22. Forces the teacher to think through the entire course;
23. Facilitates decisions regarding accreditation of educational institutions and programs, programs of study for individual students, and courses to be included in degree programs.

Another interesting discussion of why the e-syllabus is such a "big deal" is provided by the University of Tennessee at Chattanooga Teaching Resource Center (Syllabus Construction, http://www.utc.edu/Teaching-Resource-Center/syllabus.html ).    While there is some overlap with the above, they also share with the reader a number of other key reasons. A syllabus:

1. Gives students information to decide whether or not they want to continue the course;
2. Is a way for you to introduce yourself to your students;
3. Is an opportunity to explain why the course should be taken;
4. Helps you as a teacher to plan the course;
5. Provides a record of your teaching career;
6. Can help students organize their learning;
7. Prevents misunderstandings about grading, due dates, etc.
8. Can provide important information for administrators;
9. Shows that you have spent a lot of time and effort in planning the course; and
10. Communicates to students that you care about teaching and that you value their time.

We will further discuss many of these observations under "benefits to the teacher" and "benefits to the students."

**The use of dynamic and multi-dimensional media in your e-syllabus**

In the "good old days" going back thousands of years, a typical syllabus was little more then a menu of activities and books to be read during some defined period of time.    It was a static, one-way communication of times, dates and activities from the teacher to her or his students. Revision was a last minute activity; time to change the dates, add a couple of the readings, and don't forget that Spring Break eliminates these two class periods. Today all the rules have changed!

Because of the availability of multiple communication technologies, the e-syllabus has become a dynamic, interactive, multi-media course manual.    The e-syllabus facilitates your ability to make changes throughout the semester as conditions change. Read a good article? Drop it in as a digital file as the current event for you class next week. Need to attend a committee meeting during office hours?  Check to make sure no student is signed up and note under flash announcements that you will not be available for that hour. Need to provide the students with a last minute chart or diagram?  Create it in PowerPoint and drop a link to it in your Daily Assignment Description (DAD).  Are your first year architecture students still having difficulty understanding alternative roof lines such as mansard, pyramid, cross gable and kicked eaves roofs?    Include a link to drawings of each, followed by photographic    examples.    (www.ag.ohio-state.edu/~ati_cons/roofs/ roofpage.htm)  You are no longer controlled by something you created on paper before the semester starts – you are back in the driver's seat.

New technologies provide you with the opportunity to create an electronic bulletin board, establish pre-class asynchronous discussion groups, synchronous chat rooms, shared group electronic space, add sound, animation, video, audio, telephony, links to graduate assistants; the list goes on and on.  Online hotlinks to Internet resources facilitates the sharing of information never before available.  You can create an electronic bookshelf, practice exams, a confidential grade book, e-suggestion box and online forms to be complete by the students; the only limits are your imagination!  In one course (Marketing in Russia, including onsite visit) the author developed an electronic scavenger hunt in Russia, complete with maps and "treasurers" to find in St. Petersburg and Moscow.  Students were also able to practice their Russian, hear correct pronunciation, and see pictures of the objects. They were even able to go shopping or review the new Russian constitution.    Another colleague of the author created interactive student teams in the USA and Western Europe to test new product concepts. A third colleague created an "inverted classroom" within their e-syllabus.  The e-syllabus included 40 hours of PowerPoint presentations, complete with audio, plus daily exercises, charts, readings and discussion questions. The cognitive materials were to be completed prior to the class period, while the very challenging exercises and discussion questions were conducted in the class.

Questions were answered concerning the materials and small learning groups were a common class structure.

With increasing broadband, more technologically sophisticated incoming students, and high-speed communication technologies more broadly available on and off campus, the future potential of your e-syllabus "boggles the mind." The future is ours to explore to the benefit of our students and us.

**Benefits to the students of near distance learning e-syllabus**

Assuming you are responsive to the needs and wants of your primary target customers, your students, it is important to determine if an e-syllabus will result in a more meaningful learning experience. If it is not read or used by your students, it still has value to you in terms of organizing your thoughts, but may not be perceived to have value by the students. Therefore it is critical that you not only create a professional e-syllabus, but that you successfully stimulate its continual use by your students.

One of the most important functions of an e-syllabus is that it allows students to first, decide if they wish to take your course (assuming it is an elective) and second as a planning tool. They can anticipate when papers and projects are due. They know the nature and timing of the exams. If they have questions or need help, they can interact electronically with the teacher, graduate assistant or other students via email, discussion groups, bulletin boards or chat rooms. It acts as a cognitive road map for the student. From the e-syllabus they can determine the courses mission, goals and objectives, how it fits with their program of study, the rules required to effectively and efficiently complete the course of study, and the assessment tools that will be used to measure their level of achievement. If well written, it will answer most FAQ[s] that might, or should, have been asked by the students. It also acts as an electronic information resource center, containing hotlinks and digital copies of articles, lecture notes, exercises, and Internet sites. An additional benefit to students is that it commits the teacher to specific behaviors. If the e-syllabus indicates that the teacher will not make deductions for up to "x" class absences, this represents a *good faith agreement* between the two parties. For most students, "known" is better than "unknown" outcomes. Finally, it makes our professional discipline alive, dynamic, interactive and relevant. Things that the students see on TV, read in newspapers, magazines or the Internet, can be introduced into the course within a matter of days.

## Benefits to the teacher of near distance learning e-syllabus

"As professionals, instructors should expect to be fully accountable for what how they teach, and this should be reflected in the quality of the course outline" (Harriet W. Sheridan Center for Teaching and Learning – Michael Woolcock). Although some teachers consider themselves "free agents" and their classroom their own personal fiefdom, this simply is not true. Whether you work in a state supported or private educational institutional, you have multiple stakeholders who rightfully influence how and what you teach. Your courses or corporate training programs are almost always part of a larger mosaic and must effectively and efficiently develop selected knowledge and skill sets. You are dependent upon the knowledge and skills of your students as they enter your class, and your colleagues can only succeed in their roles if you have properly prepared "their" students. A professional e-syllabus is essential to the fulfillment of these obligations.

There are also numerous accountability and assessment mechanisms in place to encourage the development of professional e-syllabi. Often e-syllabi are shared with your colleagues, allowing formal or informal peer pressure to change behavior. Teaching Portfolios are required in many educational institutions, and the heart of any portfolio is your e-syllabus. Promotion, tenure and merit salary increases will, in part, reflect the quality of your e-syllabus.

Probably the most important reasons for the development and execution of a professional near distance learning e-syllabus is your intrinsic desire to be the best teacher you can be, and to provide your students with the best learning experience possible. You have chosen the field of education because it permits you to create and share knowledge and skills with others. A professional e-syllabus is one element of this commitment to excellence.

Lastly, a professional e-syllabus allows an instructor to make continuous refinements and adjustments to the document throughout the semester. While you must have the structure in terms of mission, values and vision, it is possible to add individual daily assignments over the term of the course. Let the students know that you will be modifying the original daily content based upon their demonstrated needs. Encourage their suggestions in a timely manner. In a four or five month period, you are bound to come up with refinements in individual daily assignments that are even better then your initial thoughts.

**IT and near distance learning in the classroom**

"In a national study conducted by the Center for Applied Special Technology in 1996, students with online access [to course syllabi and resources] showed significantly higher scores on measures of information management, communications, and presentation of ideas than the control group even though both groups had computers and software." He concluded that "students with access to educational technology showed positive gains in achievement on researcher-constructed tests, standardized tests, and national tests. The above-mentioned research indicates that technology and telecommunications, when used in combination with appropriate learning strategies, technology-proficient faculty and students, sufficient technology systems, and student access, can positively affect learning." (Schacfer, 1999)

Information technology (IT) has become a key component of today's business world and college-level business education (Alavi, Wheeler, and Calacich 1995; Alavi, Yoo, and Vogel,1997; Bilmoria 1999). As the educational marketplace becomes more competitive, educators must employ technology to improve their teaching (Ferrell 1995; Smart, Kelley and Conant 1999). "Additionally, the use of IT in the classroom can promote more efficient teaching and better learning (Benbunan Fich 1999). Students exposed to computer-enhanced curricula will be better prepared to manage and use information technologies when they start their business careers (Dickson and Segars, 1999).

From the above citations it is clear that the use of a professional e-syllabus has the potential to improve the learning environment while simultaneously increasing the student's information management skills.

Besides these advantages to our students, there are a number of technology and communication advantages for each of us. This development of instructional and course technology within an e-syllabus increases our flexibility and student – faculty, faculty – student, and student – student communications (McCorkle, D.E, 2001)." In addition to teaching students how to use technology for making real-world business decisions, marketing educator's use technology for the facilitation of classroom learning. Most university faculty and students have access to their own e-mail accounts and university-sponsored server space for creating their own Web sites and bulletin boards. These technologies provide new and sometimes more efficient and effective methods for faculty-to-student as well as student-to-student communication." (Atwong and Hugstad 1997;Lawson,

White and Dimitriadis 1998; McNeilly and Ranney 1998; Ragothaman and Hoadley 1997; Siegel 1996).

Even beyond the classroom environment, technology is supporting our research and information sharing needs with colleagues. "Technology can also help faculty become better academicians. Thanks to e-mail, communications with distant colleagues has never been easier. E-mail attachments of word-processing documents enhance the opportunities for coauthored research and speed up the submission, review, and publishing process for academic conferences and journals. The Internet and the Web provide easier access to university libraries from around the world and the opportunity to quickly search and explore new research opportunities. Course Web sites allow other faculty to monitor course design and syllabi for ideas and improvement of their own courses, while corporate web sites provide a wealth of information and examples to improve instruction and course currency, as well as student interest" ( Mc Corkle, D.E.,2000 ; Syllabi Collection on International Relations http://userpage.fu-berlin.de/~osifub/Syllabi.htm).

The use of IT in the classroom through your e-syllabus therefore provdes a win-win opportunity. It improves the information management of your students ; facilitates your professional dissemination of information, communication, knowledge and skills in the classroom ; and permits the sharing of classroom innovations across your department, division, university, the United States, and literally across the world. For example, the author has relied on 120 other faculty members' e-syllabi for inspiration and action ideas as can be seen in Appendix A : Part 2.

**The e-syllabus as a communication medium**

Historically, syllabi contained only words in a written hard copy format and were unidirectional in nature from the teacher to the student. It was a static document, created prior to the beginning of a semester or quarter, and the only changes possible were announcements in class. New technologies now permit entirely new pedagogies, dynamic two-way communication, instant access to people and information, and learning opportunities simply not possible twn years ago. Through the use of online discussion groups, bulletin boards, and chat rooms, a teacher can multiply many-fold the participation opportunities (floor time) for individual students. Through these media the teacher can focus in on the areas of interest and concern of the student. The teacher can quickly identify problem areas of knowledg or skill that are being faced by the class or by individual students. It is a feedback loop operating 24/7.

The use of an e-syllabus also opens the door to the world as the source of expertise for you and your students. Information contained in Scotland, the Library of Congress, a 10K report of Disney, or a recent article in the *Wall Street Journal* is at your fingertips. You can make available to your students lecture notes, PowerPoint presentations, streaming video, audio, photos, animations, and more for your Art History class. Have your student conduct primary and secondary marketing research on line. Schedule a teleconference, chat room or online email relationship with an expert on digital photography at Apple. Not a problem!

A third vital communication tool served by your e-syllabus is its use as a scheduling tool. You can post your office hours and have students actually reserve specific times. This allows the teacher to avoid queues at the door and wasted time when no students need your face-to-face help. It also saves your student time by guaranteeing them a specific time when they can come in for help. It is particularly useful in both corporate settings and high schools were every individual has a unique schedule of activities.

**Legal issues and the copyrighting of materials**

We live in a litigious environment. It sometimes feels as if our students are all lawyers looking for loopholes. A comprehensive and professional syllabus can greatly reduce misunderstandings and therefore possible grievances or legal actions. It's all there in the syllabus. "Late" means after the close of the class period in which the assignment is due. Missed pop quizzes are recorded as zeros. Sorry. No make-ups. If you miss seven classes for any reason, you will be dropped with a failing grade. An "A-" is from 90% to 92.49%. What do you mean by dishonestly? This can be particularly difficult in a culturally diverse classroom where there are many different meanings of dishonesty. More later.

Is an e-syllabus actually a legally binding contract? The answer to this question is, no, not now, perhaps if covered under good teaching practices in a Student Manual or University Bulletin, and probably yes in the future. A review of federal law in the United States from 1971 to June of 2001 provides us with approximately 19 relevant major court actions under three different statues and laws. The most comprehensive finding occurred in 1972 and "recognized that catalogues, manuals, handbooks, student manuals, registration materials, bulletins, and regulations of the institution made available to the student, are part of the contract" and therefore subject to breach of contract claims. (Zumbrun v. University of Southern California, 25 Cal. App. 3d 1, 1972)   These findings were supported by actions in the following cases: Bradshaw v. Rawlings, 612 F.2d 135(3rd Cir.19790; Mangla v. Brown University, 135 F.33d 80 (1st Cir. 198); Fellheimer v. Middlebury College, 869 F. Supp. 238 (D. Vermont 1994); Lerner v. Ravenswood Hospital Medical Center, 1999 WL 1267710 (N.D. Ill. 1999), 1999 U.S. Dist. LEXIS 19804); Coddington v. Adelphi University, 45 F.Supp. 2d 211 (E.D. N.Y. 1999); Govan v. Trustees of Boston University, 66 F.Supp. 2d 74 (D. Mass. 1999 citing Russell v. Salve Regina College, 890 F. 2d 484 (1st Cir. 1989).   The word "syllabi" was not included in any of the decisions above, but might be considered a manual, handbook or student manual in some future action.

Violations of "e-syllabus like" educational materials have also been taken to court under **Educational Malpractice** law. "Courts have generally been willing to recognize that they should only intervene in matters arising in an academic context where an action was arbitrary or capricious." *Doherty v Southern Cross College of Optometry, 862 F .2d 570 (6th Cir 1988); Rothman v Emory University, 1994 WL 113080 (N.D Ill, 1994), 1994 Dist LEXIS 4002; Bleicher v University of Cincinnati College of Medicine, 604 N E. 2nd 783 (Ohio Ct App 1992);Ewing Regents of University of Michigan v. Ewing, 474 U S 214,226, 88 L. Ed. 2d 523, 106 S. Ct. (1985); Elliott v. University of Cincinnati, 1999 WL 430626 (Ohio Ct App. 1999), 1999 Ohio App LEXIS 2988, Armstrong v. Wright State University, 724 N.E. 2d 881 (Ct.Clms. Ohio 1999).*   In the case Ross v. Creighton University "…which combined educational malpractice and breach of contract claims, the court distinguished between true breach of contract claims and educational malpractice claims.   The court stated that breach of contract claims that attack the general quality of an education are barred in the same way as an education malpractice claim because to evaluate the claim, a court   would have to evaluate the course of instruction and the methodology adopted by the institution"(Ross v. Creighton University, 957 F 2d 410 7th Cir. 1992).

While most actions against universities in the past 30 years have been under contract or educational malpractice law, seven suits have been brought under the Consumer Sales Practice Act.   All of these have resulted in action favorable to the educational institution.   The broadest finding was by the Court of Appeals of Ohio, 10th District, Franklin County of the case Malone et al Appellants v. Academy of Court Reporting decided 12/31/90. In the court's opinion, "The quality of the education and qualifications of the teachers employed by the private school are concerns not for the courts, but rather for the State Education Department and its commissioner." Actions taken under the Consumer Sales Practice Act by the Federal Trade Commission, Supreme Court of Ohio and Office of the Attorney General have had similar outcomes.

From the above we can fairly safely assume that, as of June of 2001, a syllabus or e-syllabus only falls under the umbrella of a *good faith agreement,* and violation of terms specified or omitted from the document have not been subject to litigation. However, this is not true concerning action related to university or college specified "good teaching practices". While what is a good teaching practice, as normally specified in a Student Handbook, differs by college or university, it is very important to check the good teaching practices published by your university. Indirectly, as these often appear in a student manual, they may become subject to both grievance and legal action under breach of contract provisions.

The second issue to consider is the copyrighting of your syllabus and the copyright regulations of materials digitally reproduced for limited distribution or hotlinks to copyrighted materials. This is an area under transition in which changes are likely to occur in the upcoming year or two. As a general concept, *The Digital Millennium Copyright Act of 1998* protects faculty and graduate students (but not undergraduates) from copyright violations for linking to copyrighted material legally available on the Internet. However, teachers and trainers are expected to remove copyrighted materials upon request by the copyright holder. Software and music are not included under the above conditions. (http://www.educause.edu/ir/library/html/cem9913.html )

It is also legal to change the format of material that is copyrighted from print to digital format if distribution is limited to students in your class for a defined period of time. There are also some limits on the amount of material from a single source, but this is not normally a problem for individual articles. (Fair Use Doctrine http://www.arl.org/info/frn/copy/fairuse.html )

It is recommended that you place a copyright notation on the home page of your e-syllabus, including the symbol, your name, and the statement that this copyright relates to all materials original to the faculty member and present or linked directly or indirectly to the home page. While this will not provide 100% copyright protection, it is the best you can do while the courts sort out ownership rights of near distance learning e-syllabi. This should stop your notes from being sold commercially by third parties.

**The Teaching Portfolio, assessment & accountability**

The e-syllabus is the foundation of teaching portfolios, a document increasingly used by colleges and universities as summative and normative documentation in assessing teaching effectiveness and efficiency. E-syllabi are also an important document required for all accreditation reviews at the high school and college level to determine if the defined mission is being executed within the classroom. E-syllabi and teaching portfolios are also often part of a faculty member's Annual, Tenure and Promotion Reports, commonly used to determine salary increases, promotion and the granting of tenure.

Since the early 1990s state legislators, trustees and regents are taking an increasingly active role in the measurement of educational outcomes. To the extent e-syllabus define their course mission, values and vision in a manner consistent with that of the university, and they identify assessment mechanisms that are rigorous and objective, the e-syllabus will provide strong support for funding by the state for your academy. It can also be a valuable and required input into the proposal of new undergraduate and graduate majors, minors, thematic sequences, capstones and core courses (Garavalia, L.S., 1999).

In many academic institutions, student evaluations in individual courses are refined down a couple of numbers that administrators interpret as indicators of effective teaching. This unidimensional measure is often found as unacceptable by faculties, who have a strong preference for multiple measures providing objective convergent validity. "The familiar complaint of relying on student evaluations alone as the measure of effective teaching can be at least partially obviated by including course outlines [E-syllabus] as a major component of one's overall teaching portfolio. (Harriet W. Sheridan Center for Teaching and Learning/Michael Woolcock, no date) The syllabus can also be used during parent-teacher meetings in HS to clarify the nature of the course for all stakeholders. This is one major step to achieving convergent validity.

**Think "course guidelines" as you prepare your e-syllabus**

As you go through the nine steps necessary before you actually create your e-syllabus, think about what you wish to communicate to the students, what you want to make available to them to achieve your (and hopefully their) behavioral objectives, and finally what are things students want to know. What you are really preparing is are electronic course guidelines. This is not a one or two page outline of dates, topics and activities. It is much more. Teaching is a huge responsibility you have taken upon yourself; something that can potentially change the entire lives of other persons. You are about to open the windows to knowledge. You should be exhilarated…and frightened by this awesome opportunity. Take the time to carefully think about the following nine-step program. Make revisions. Share it with your colleagues and get feedback. Revise. Test it in the classroom and then revise it again. When you have prepared the absolutely best syllabus you can, remember that it is a living document in a dynamic, ever changing field, and will probably require minor revisions weekly. When the semester is over and you have carefully reviewed feedback from various stakeholders, start the revision process as soon as possible. You can and will change lives through the creation and execution of a professional e-syllabus!

PART TWO
NINE  KEY STEPS TO TAKE BEFORE ACTUALLY WRITING
YOUR E-SYLLABUS

**Step 1: Write down your personal values, attitudes, beliefs, preferences, priorities and philosophy of teaching, learning and assessment.**

Why should students attend colleges or universities? What is the role of higher education as a change agent? Is your function to be the *sage on the stage* or *the guide on the side* (Gibson, 1996)? How much responsibility should the students take for their own learning? How much structure and control do you desire in the classroom? Is your focus on teaching or really on learning? What kind of a role model do you wish to be? Do you have any personal agendas that you wish to advocate to the students? Do you prefer small groups, lectures, discussions or case studies? How do you wish to balance knowledge acquisition with skill development? How do you feel about teaching versus research and service? What is your level of technological sophistication? These and dozens of other questions need to be answered before you can start the preparation of an e-syllabus. Some of these answers you will want to share with your students in the e-syllabus under *Teaching philosophy*, while others will be more reflective and introspective in nature.

"A course plan demonstrates our values and beliefs about higher education in general, and what we believe about our roles as teachers, specifically." (The Teaching and Learning Center of the University of Nebraska-Lincoln web page on *Planning a College Course* http://www.unl.edu/teaching/Planning Course.html).

For example, let's look at the concept of a learning-centered e-syllabus versus a teacher-centered e-syllabus. "The learning centered syllabus addresses student learning and responds to the question: What do students need to know in order to derive maximum benefit from this educational experience" (Grunert, Judith, 1997). What balance of theory and application will best serve your students personally and professionally? What would you like them to retain for at least five years? "Focusing on learning rather than teaching requires a shift from an overview of what you as the instructor will cover to consideration of what your students need in order to be successful learners. This change in focus can also affect the student's role in your course. Accepting responsibility for their own learning can be difficult for students who have been educated as most have, as passive listeners and is particularly difficult for some international students" (Grunert, Judith, 1997).

If you believe in this learning center approach, you will need to structure the course to provide additional learning discovery opportunities through projects, role-playing, debates, primary and secondary research, cases or discussion groups. There will also be less spoon-feeding of information. Some of your behavioral goals will probably include: to develop life long learners, the ability to discover and filter facts from opinions, skills in information acquisition, and higher level thinking skills such as synthesis and evaluation.

Another decision you will need to make is, how much of your personality, values, beliefs and ethics should be woven into the fabric of the class. Will you address social issues of diversity and gender stereotypes into your Consumer Behavior or International Marketing class? Should you introduce ethical discussions into case studies related to new product development? Will you limit your advising role to questions of fact, or will you provide personal career and life assistance?

A third major philosophical decision you need to make relates to student assessment. Do you believe in the "normal curve" in determining the number of "As" and "Fs" to issue? Are your performance standards high and therefore very few "As" and "Bs" are to be given in your class?  On the other hand, do you take pleasure in giving as many high grades as possible, indicating that your students' knowledge and skills are very good to excellent relative to your standards for their performance?  How important are written and oral communication skills and how, if at all, will they be incorporated into the assessment process.

Values and goals will have a direct impact on both the content and pedagogy used and prescribed in an e-syllabus.  As advised by the experts at the Technology and Learning Center at the University of Nebraska-Lincoln:

"A. If it is to make the world a better place, you'll want to use contemporary social issues to help students learn their roles in accomplishing this goal.

B. If it is to teach students to think effectively, you'll need to plan student interaction employing the intellectual skills of observing, classifying, applying, analyzing, and evaluating.

C. If it demands systematic instructional processes, you'll need to specify course goals and objectives clearly, with the processes designed to achieve them.

D. If it is to provide students with the ability to earn a living as productive citizens, you'll need to include vocational knowledge and skills.

E. If it is to engage students in personally enriching experiences, then you need to select individualized content so students will discover themselves as unique individuals and develop personal autonomy.

F. If it should emphasize the great ideas, products and discoveries of the human mind, you must select content from the discipline to illuminate major ideas and concepts of important thinkers.

G. If it should help students clarify their beliefs and values to provide guidance in their lives, you must plan exercises that consider the merits of alternative values."

A final example relates to your assumption about your students, their motivations and abilities.  Are they at school because they want to play sports, make a lot of money, to find a spouse, because of family pressure, to play and have a good time, because of state requirements, or do they possess a real thirst for knowledge and skills?  What will you need to do to motivate them to learn?   How important will entertainment be in the classroom?  Do you position your teaching to the best student, the weakest student or the student in the middle…and where is that middle?

Most of us do not give adequate consideration to the above types of philosophical issues prior to the preparation of our e-syllabus.

However, your answers to the above questions, and many more, are vital to the preparation of the professional e-syllabus.

**Step 2: What is the role of the course within the institution?**

Your e-syllabus is usually dependent upon the courses that the students have taken prior to your class and the courses that will follow. Is your course part of the core? If so, the course must make links to a variety of disciplines and will more likely emphasize breadth over depth. On the other hand, if this is the capstone course for seniors, you can expect higher level learning skills, a foundation of knowledge in multiple disciplines, a higher level of maturity, and the capacity for greater self-directed learning, problem solving and decision making.

A second question that needs to be asked is, "is this course part of a common curriculum, major, minor, thematic sequence, concentration, divisional core or free elective?" If part of one of your departmental sequences, your colleagues may have specified certain knowledge or skills that should be acquired in your class. There may even be common exams. The course might have been designated as writing or oral intensive, technology intensive, or one of the courses in which teams and/or negotiations should be practiced. All of these will obviously influence your e-syllabus.

**Step 3: Determine physical, technological, courseware, time, administrative and other parameters influencing the e-syllabus.**

**Physical considerations**

Almost all high schools, colleges and universities are dealing with balancing the demand of students and the availability of "appropriate" classrooms. If you are teaching a section of *Chemistry or Biology* with 450 students and limited graduate student support, the physical parameters of students, classroom and time will dictate teaching pedagogies. If there are no tiered case rooms or group classrooms, cases, small group projects, the inverted classroom, use of focus groups, etc. becomes more difficult if not impossible. Because most schools are trying to maximize their use of available classroom hours, teachers many be forced into spaces with inadequate facilities, classes that are too large for desired pedagogical methods, poorly equipped for maximum learning, or at hours found undesirable by both the professor and their students. Teaching statistics, math or music at 8:00 am as a required course for sophomores can be a challenge!

## Technology and courseware

If your school is on the backside of the technology curve, has few classrooms that are multimedia ready, limited LAN or WAN student access, and doesn't support commercial courseware, you will be severely limited in your use of an e-syllabus. Even the presence of dated hardware and software in faculty offices, on divisional servers, and student labs can make the creation and day-to-day use of an e-syllabus fairly painful. Fortunately, a great majority of colleges and universities have made great strides in the use of technology, particularly in both short and pure distance learning. "According to Steinberg and Wyatt 2000, 'More than one-third of all colleges and universities in the United States already offer distance learning, as it is called; by 2002, four of every five are expected to do so." (Eastman, J.K.,2001) According to the National Center for Education Statistics, between 1997-98 and intended use in 2000-2001, in 4-year public institutions, there will be an increase from 78% to 90% who offer distance learning courses. This represents a 15.3% increase. In private four-year institutions for these same years, the increase will be from 19% to 41%, a 115% increase. The combined public and private four-year institutions will increase from 870 out of 1660 to 1390 (52.4% to 83.7%); an overall % increase of 59.7%.

"Technology can also help faculty become better academicians. Thanks to e-mail, communications with distant colleagues has never been easier. E-mail attachments of word-processing documents enhance the opportunities for coauthored research and speed up the submission, review, and publishing process for academic conferences and journals. The Internet and the Web provide easier access to university libraries from around the world and the opportunity to quickly search and explore new research opportunities. Course Web sites allow other faculty to monitor course design and syllabi for ideas and improvement of their own courses, while corporate web sites provide a wealth of information and examples to improve instruction and course currency, as well as student interest" (McCorkle, J.F.,2001).

The use of appropriate technology by your students in response to your e-syllabus can positively affect student learning. "In a national study conducted by the Center for Applied Special Technology in 1996, students with online access showed significantly higher scores on measures of information management, communications, and presentation of ideas than the control group even though both groups had computers and software (Schacter 1999). He concluded that students with access to education technology showed positive gains in achievement on researcher-constructed tests, standardized tests, and national tests. The above mentioned research indicates that technology and telecommunications, when used in combination with appropriate learning strategies, technology-proficient faculty and students, sufficient technology systems, and student access, can positively affect learning" (www/jme p.48).

A secondary, but important outcome of incorporating technology into your e-syllabus, either through your web page or courseware, is that it helps students understand how technology facilitates learning and decision-making. ""In addition to teaching students how to use technology for making real-world business decisions, marketing educators use technology for the facilitation of classroom learning. Most high school, university faculty and students have access to their own e-mail accounts and university-sponsored server space for creating their own Web sites and bulletin boards. These technologies provide new and sometimes more efficient and effective methods for faculty-to-student as well as student-to-student communication (Atwong and Hugstad 1997;Lawson, White and Dimitriadis 1998; McNeilly and Ranney 1998; Ragothaman and Hoadley 1997; Siegel 1996; McCorkle, J.F., 2001).

The use of courseware such as Blackboard, Lotus Learning Space, WBT Systems, TopClass 5, and Oncourse, have greatly eased the load on faculty to learn web page editing programs to build e-syllabus. A single faculty member can adopt some of these, while others require an entire campus to adopt the course management software. Most of the commands in courseware are fairly intuitive, the software forgiving, and the learning curve less than one-half a day. While a technical discussion of the alternative course management software is beyond the scope of this book, it is recommended that you explore whatever software becomes the standard for your campus. All of the above can handle information distribution (hot links, announcements), communications (e-mail, discussion groups, chat rooms) and class management (announcements, track attendance, recording progress, calculating grades, etc.). It can save you lots of time in the creation of your e-syllabus.

**Administrative and time commitments**

It would be nice to say that the preparation and regular updating of an e-syllabus takes no more time than it takes for a written syllabus distributed on day one. Nice but inaccurate. The first time it will take <u>much more time</u> to create and maintain you e-syllabus than a traditional printed syllabus. A study by Palloff and Pratt in 1999 (Palloff, R.M., 1999) indicates the time commitment to be somewhere between two and three times (6.5-7.5hours/week to 18-19 hours/week). However, each semester the process becomes more and more time efficient. After a couple of semesters, you will be unwilling to go back!

**Step 4: Know your target market and other stakeholders.**

"As instructors, placing your students' learning and development as a priority means that you must consider their varied educational needs, interests, and purposes as you determine the content and structure of your course" (IBTME/JME p.1).

Who will be taking this course...and why? What is students' existing knowledge bases or skill sets? Are they full time or part time students? Are they seventh graders, middle management, traditional college students or adult learners? How many hours per week are they willing to put into your class outside of actual classroom time? What are their educational, maturity and intellectual levels? How comfortable are they with technology? Do they have broadband or slow computer access to your e-syllabus from their homes or do most operate from the work place, dorm rooms or computer labs? What are their professional and educational backgrounds? What is the students' interest level in the course content? The answers to all these questions are EXTREMELY important in thinking about the design of your course. You will only become frustrated if you design an e-syllabus that entails six hours of homework a week if the students mostly work full-time and are adult learners. If 50% of your students will be non-majors taking this course as a free elective and there are no prerequisites, you will need to build in more tutorials, introductory reference materials, an appendix of technical terms, and will need to move more slowly through complex core concepts.

You should also be aware of the expectations of your students, particularly as they relate to your e-syllabus. According to J. D. Leeds, University of Tennessee, students want an e-syllabus that is: concise, presents the most important ideas first, makes expectations clear, lists all known dates, is specific about the grading process, calls attention to objectives, identifies how the course relates to the student's lives, and describes the consequences for not following course rules (Leeds, J.D., U. of Tennessee, http://www.utc.edu/Teaching-Resource-Center/ syllabus.html ).

Another variable to take into consideration are the students' levels of technological sophistication and the availability of computer access to your e-syllabus on a 24/7 basis. While many of your students will be very comfortable with today's computer technology, some students may not be able to handle the demands of your e-syllabus. "One marketing professor found that 10% to 20% of her students (based upon written student comments) over a three-semester time frame were uncomfortable with the technology" (Siegel, 1996). Another found that undergraduate students in a capstone marketing course gave the lowest ratings of their skill sets to those skills used in obtaining technology-based sources of information (Miller and Mangold, 1996).

A final consideration is the need of the other relevant stakeholders such as the student's parents or guardians, potential employers, alumni, principals, legislators (for public institutions), administrators, colleagues and yourself.   If potential employers are looking for additional levels of expertise in written and oral communication skills, information management technology, leadership, negotiation and time management, these are things that you should consider integrating into your e-syllabus.  If legislators or trustees are demanding higher levels of "productivity" while supplying reduced financial resources, larger sections with small discussion labs lead by graduate assistants may become necessary. If employers and graduate schools are demanding higher grades for consideration, is grade inflation acceptable to allow the students to be competitive in the marketplace?   If your enrollment and funding is determined by success on standardized exams in K-12, curriculum and ways-of-knowing must be consistent with passing the standardized exams.

Obviously you, your colleagues and the college or university administrators will have an influence on the construction of your e-syllabus.  Certain mandates may have come down "from above" concerning institutional mission, values and vision. Maybe your course is designated as vertically or horizontally integrated within or beyond your discipline. Is there a strong suggestion that issues of diversity be addressed in all classes? Is your own personal and professional interest in biodiversity, with particular interest on environmental sustainability? Won't this impact consciously or unconsciously how you teach that *Botany* course?

In marketing we always start with the needs and wants of our primary stakeholders that we can satisfy effectively, efficiently...and at a profit. There is no reason we should not adopt the same philosophy as we create our e-syllabus!

**Step 5: Define your course mission, values and vision.**

Do we teach what we preach? If so, we really have no choice but to define for our students, and ourselves, the mission (and scope), values and vision of our course. Not to do so would be like driving a high speed Cigarette™ off-shore racing boat at 90 knots per hour on a foggy day using a 10 foot pole to make sure you don't run into anything. Not a good idea! These (the mission, values and vision statements) will be incorporated into our final e-syllabus.

Your mission statement should be a "universal yet meaningful expression of the course's intended operational scope, its sense of social responsibility, and its future direction.    If teaching a *French Literature* course what are the operational parameters of the course and will social issues and the ethics be actively addressed.  Will French Art CD-ROMs begin to be integrated into the course?    The goals (qualitative   expression   of   desired   outcomes)   and   objectives (quantitative expression of desired outcomes) will be highlighted under e-syllabus Behavioral Objectives.  Within the mission statement we must carefully consider the SCOPE of our e-syllabus.  We have all faced the difficult decision of what to include and **what to exclude** from our courses.   There is always more knowledge and skills you would like to share with your students than there is time in the semester.

After the mission and scope statement, the next steps are brief value and vision statements.  The value statement identifies the roles, rights and responsibilities to the stakeholders.  Your answers to the questions concerning the target market and stakeholders should provide you with input into a fairly concise values statement.   The vision statement should include a general blueprint for accomplishing the organizations mission, goals and objectives. This will require a blending of the class structure (part of step 6), plus the instructional strategies (step 9), all boiled down into two to three sentences. Appendix C provides an example of a mission, value and vision statement, as used in a senior capstone *Marketing Strategy* course.

**Step 6: Determine your desired course environment and structures.**

What type of course environment do you wish to create in your classroom? Some teachers are most comfortable in a highly structured environment where each class sequence, mood and content are planned in advance.  Other teachers prefer a less structured environment were designed learning objectives for the day can be achieved in a variety of ways.

Another dimension of the classroom environment relates to the desired relationship between the faculty member and her or his students.   This starts with how you are addressed (Professor's last name, first name or other), how you address your students, and the "feel" of the class, both within and outside the classroom. This is not something that just happens, but something that can be managed by the professor and should be engineered within the e-syllabus. A good example can be seen in the syllabus for Religion 2 at Central Catholic High School under *Classroom Procedures* and *Additional Policies* (http://www.cchs-satx.org/academics/religion2syllabus.htm ).

**How will you structure your course?**

- ❖ A metaphor
- ❖ A journey
- ❖ A parable
- ❖ A sports game
- ❖ A museum
- ❖ A romance
- ❖ A concerto
- ❖ An obstacle course (above from Grunert, Judith, 1997)
- ❖ Micro to macro, or the reverse
- ❖ A time line, from past, through the present, and then the future
- ❖ A conceptual model (such as this book)
- ❖ Functional or strategic in nature
- ❖ Conceptual and theory → applied knowledge and skills
- ❖ A learning hierarchy, from simple to complex
- ❖ Integrative within and/or across business disciplines
- ❖ Vocational
- ❖ Organized around issues, dilemmas, ethical problems or value dimensions (Teaching & Learning Center – Nebraska, website)
- ❖ Level of learning (Bloom Taxonomy – See Step 9)
- ❖ Knowledge threads and skill sets
- ❖ Other structures you have found successful

There is no one structure that is generally better than all the others; you must decide based upon steps one through five, plus your own personal preferences. Different courses will dictate different structures. Sometimes evolutionary changes in your course may require you to change the structure that you have used successfully in the past. For example, maybe your Evidence Based Medicine class has always been taught using functional, conceptual and applied formats. However, this semester you are changing the course to active use case-based learning. This may be done more effectively using actual clinical "stories" including learning issues and additional reference materials (http://www.int-med.uiowa.edu/education/Clerkship/CBLHyper tension.htm). This is a very important decision and will influence everything that appears in your syllabus.

**Step 7: Prepare a list of your Behavioral Learning Objectives and what students should be able to know and do.**

"Few instructors conceive of their course as the medium which links student learning to the attainment of the department's and the university's mission statement. The course outline [e-syllabus] is in fact part of a four-way agreement between instructor, students, the department, and the institution or corporation. An important aspect of thinking pedagogically entails making clear and explicit connections between course and departmental objectives, between departments and the university mission statement, and most importantly and immediately, between the instructor's goals and the students' expectations. If those connections are made successfully, then mutual expectations are established right from the start, and both teaching and learning become more effective" (Harriet W. Sheridan Center for Teaching and Learning/Michael Woolcock).

"Clearly stated aims [goals] and objectives are the foundation stone on which the edifice of your course outline is then constructed. Aims [goals] are broad statements identifying the general educational outcomes you want a graduate of your course to be able to display, while objectives are the concrete measure by which these will be realized, [measured] and are usually expressed as relationships between specific concepts. The extent to which students achieve the course objectives is the extent to which they realize the aims of the course, and is the measure of your teaching effectiveness." (Harriet W. Sheridan Center for Teaching and Learning/Michael Woolcock )   From the above two quotes related to mission statements, goals and objectives, one can see that behavioral objectives are a natural outcome, and part of this process of creating an e-syllabus.

For those of you with a background in educational methods, the term "behavioral objective" is probably familiar lexicon. However, for many of us fine arts, the natural sciences or humanities, this many be a new concept. Behavioral Objectives relate to cognitive, affective and psychomotor outcomes that are desired within a specific course or program of learning. The cognitive desired outcomes are those points of information or knowledge we want our students to acquire, plus the way we wish them to be able to process this information. Examples include models, concepts, theories, facts, structures, vocabulary, and disciplinary building blocks and tools. They also include skills such as teamwork, communications, negotiation, leadership, problem solving, critical thinking, information creation and management, management risk taking and uncertainty, creativity, etc. The phrases we tie to knowledge and skills are extremely important and our assessment tools must be consistent with these terms. Examples of commonly used terms relating to cognitive objectives include:

Figure 2

❖ To read and summarize...
❖ To synthesize...
❖ To analyze..
❖ To classify ..
❖ To collaborate..
❖ To compare & contrast...
❖ To compute. .
❖ To define...
❖ To demonstrate...
❖ To direct...
❖ To designate...
❖ To discuss...
❖ To display ..
❖ To evaluate..
❖ To explain...
❖ To identify...
❖ To infer...
❖ To integrate...
❖ To interpret...
❖ To justify...
❖ To list...
❖ To model...
❖ To name...
❖ To organize...

❖ To outline
❖ To report ..
❖ To respond
❖ To solicit.
❖ To state. .
❖ To synthesize
❖ To compute and interpret .
❖ To diagram in a CPM and flow chart
❖ To evaluate and critique ..
❖ To discover
❖ To effectively communicate. .

(Some of these were taken from the Harriet W. Sheridan Center for Teaching and Learning/Michael Woolcock.)

A similar list of terms can be related to the affective objectives, or how we wish our students to feel as they complete various parts of our course. Some of these might include:

Figure 3

| |
|---|
| ❖   To inspire… |
| ❖   To generate excitement and enthusiasm about… |
| ❖   To enjoy… |
| ❖   To tolerate… |
| ❖   To feel… |
| ❖   To sensitize .. |
| ❖   To commit to… |
| ❖   To have fun… |

Many of us subconsciously recognize that some of our objectives relate to feelings and emotions, but fail to make these clear to our students.

A third list of behavioral objectives relates to psychomotor skills that we want the students to acquire within our course. While these may be the most important in a trade, military or vocational school, these are rarely very important in other disciplines. Even in decision or computer sciences, most of the behavioral objectives relate to knowledge and skills and not the "eye/hand" coordination needed to hand wire…or the ability to cut a French curve in a piece of wood.

As we are communicating these behavioral objectives, we are simultaneously delineating what we want our students to be able to know and be able to do. We may want them to be able to describe, draw and label a new product life cycle curve and then apply this knowledge to Kimberly's Fresh™ Rollwipes wet toilet tissue. They should be able to identify the current stage of this product in this life cycle and predict when the maturity stage will transition into the saturation stage and why. The student's ability to do the above will be assessed through the accuracy of their prediction and the soundness of the logic supporting the prediction during a 20-minute, open notes in-class quiz. These behavioral objectives will need to appear in the syllabus and be refined into more micro terms in our daily assignments.

**Step 8: Decide upon levels of desired learning and ways of knowing.**

As you wrote your behavioral objectives you were actually indicating in our syllabus the level of knowledge and skills you wanted them to assimilate. If one refers to Bloom's taxonomy of the cognitive domains, you can see the behavioral objectives that relate to each level:

Figure 4

> Bloom's Taxonomy of the Cognitive Domain:
> http://www.ntlf.com/html/lib/suppmat/84taxonomy.htm
> A.    Knowledge (Remembering information): define, identify, label, state, list, match;
> B.    Comprehension (Explaining the meaning of information): describe, generalize, paraphrase, summarize, and estimate;
> C.    Application (Using abstractions in concrete situations): determine, chart, implement, prepare, solve, use, and develop;
> D.    Analysis (Breaking down a whole into component parts): differentiate, distinguish, discriminate, compare;
> E.    Synthesis (Putting parts together to form a new and integrated whole): create, design, plan, organize, generate;
> F.    Evaluation (Making judgments about the merits of ideas, materials, or phenomena): appraise, critique, judge, weigh, evaluate, select.

In most of our classes, it is very difficult to bring our students from the level of knowledge to evaluation in one semester. We will have to define in our own minds how far we wish to advance our students as it relates to various skill sets. Maybe basic knowledge level involving labels and definitions are acceptable for understanding the difference between department stores and a big box store; however, we will attempt to bring them to the evaluation stage relative to the use of auction web sites in B2B marketing. Another example might be Principles of European History & Art classes taught in mass sections to sophomore. In this case moving students in most functional areas from knowledge through comprehension and application would be a real challenge.

While thinking about the level of cognition desired, we will need to accommodate individual student differences in how they learn. Some may be auditory, others visual, and still others may learn by doing (kinesthetic learners).    It will take a creative mix of instructional strategies to achieve uniformly high levels of cognition.

**Step 9: Plan a variety of instructional strategies.**

All teachers have a variety of tools in their teaching bag.  Many of us learned under the lecture format, and have, at least in part, adopted this instructional strategy.  But today, it is imperative that we carefully match our teaching methods to reflect the answers to the above eight steps  "Because today's students have been surrounded by the 'vibrant impulses' of television, video, and CD games, the traditional lecture method of education lacks the necessary stimuli to keep them interested (Stansberry, 1993).  Thus, education delivery systems must address a variety of needs.  As marketers, we teach our students to recognize and serve customer needs; likewise, we must be prepared to address the changing needs of our students and our stakeholders "(Eastman, J.K., 2001).

Because of these "vibrant impulses", our students easily tire of any one instructional strategy no matter how appropriate and effective for the behavioral objectives.  Therefore, it is important to consider a variety of instructional strategies that can be used to achieve similar goals.  This issue really has two dimensions: the specific instructional strategy, and the technology and medium incorporated into its delivery. One can conduct a mock role-playing sales presentation in the class and have the other students provide oral or written feedback.  In addition, the presentation can be videotaped and self-critiques can be required. Videotape the presentations using digital facilities, place excerpts on the class e-syllabus, and have outside experts provide your students with confidential feedback.    Add teleconferencing, and allow a dialogue concerning the presentation.  Require the student presenters to use props and PowerPoint and further analyze their visual communication skills.

These nine steps have prepared you to start creating your syllabus. While there is still a lot of work to be done, if you have consciously completed these nine steps, the actual preparation of the syllabus will be much, much easier.

Figure 5
**INSTRUCTIONAL STRATEGIES = A COMBINATION OF...**

PEDAGOGIES
❖ Training
❖ Coaching
❖ Lecturing
❖ Explaining
❖ Discovery method
❖ Groups
❖ Teams
❖ Experience
❖ Reflection
❖ Debates
❖ Simulations
❖ Team projects
❖ Negotiations
❖ Case studies
❖ Role playing
❖ Experiential
❖ Observational
❖ Games (like jeopardy)
❖ Electronic Scavenger hunts

ELECTRONIC
MEDIA
❖   Hot Links
❖   Chat rooms
❖   Discussions
❖   Video
❖   Audio
❖   Internet
❖   WWW
❖   Teleconference
❖   Telephony
❖   Virtual Reality
❖   Video cameras
❖   FAX
❖   Telephone

STRUCTURES
❖   a metaphor
❖   a journey
❖   a parable
❖   a sports game
❖   a museum
❖   a romance
❖   a concerto
❖   an obstacle
    course
❖   micro to
    macro, or the
    reverse
❖   a time line,
    from past,
    through the
    present, and
    then the
    future
❖   a conceptual
    model (such
    as this book)
❖   functional or
    strategic in
    nature
❖   conceptual
    and theory →
    applied
    knowledge
    and skills
❖   a learning
    hierarchy,
    from simple
    to complex
❖   integrative
    within and/or
    across
    business
    disciplines

EQUALS THOUSANDS OF
COMBINATIONS OF INSTRUCTIONAL
STRATEGIES, ELECTRONIC MEDIA,
AND STRUCTURES

**PART THREE**
**THE ACTUAL FORMAT OF THE E-SYLLABUS**

It is now time to start to prepare your near distance learning e-syllabus. You have either written down or answered mentally the questions contained in the above nine steps and therefore have a clear understanding of the intended environment and processes that will be carried out in the classroom. Whether using courseware or your own Internet home page, there are a number of format and logistical decisions that need to be made.

Your e-syllabus should provide a cognitive map for your student that is logical and very easy to navigate. "A helpful strategy for developing both quality content and sequencing is to lay out your lecture topics into a 'conceptual map', or flow chart. This helps to clarify in your own mind whether there is a clear logic and sequence to each component of your course. Distributing such a chart early in the semester is also good for students, who may not otherwise make the necessary connections between different components of the course until later in the semester." (Harriet W. Sheridan Center for Teaching and Learning/Michael Woolcock)

In the following pages we will discuss the 24 sections that should normally be contained in your e-syllabus. The key is to create an e-syllabus that accomplishes all your objectives, while making it dynamic, interactive, simple to use, and a valuable tool to both your students and yourself. It should be comprehensive in scope and consistent in format. "In general, faculty members and students report preferring a more comprehensive syllabus. Both groups also report that flexibility is important. Syllabi should not be static documents, but should be revised as needed throughout the semester" (Garavalia, L.S., 1999).

To accomplish these objectives, it is suggested that you place the various sections in the order illustrated in the original model, starting with the header, flash announcements, and table of contents matrix, and ending with the caveat statement. The margins should be kept to a maximum of 60 and all type size should be 12 point or larger. Bold, italics, underlining, typeface and color type should be used consistently throughout the document. For example, all flash announcements added within the past 5 days should be in one color and all hyperlinks in another. Animations, audio and video should be playable on multiple software packages and versions if possible. If you use pictures, keep them small and relevant. They should be fun, appropriate and sensitive to the feelings of your students. Java should be avoided, as it is often not adequately supported by the most commonly used windows software. Your course website should only be one click away from you home page. It is suggested that you limit your fonts to those easily read by almost all computers, such as Arial or Times New Roman.

Consistent use of headings is important. All major headings for the 24 sections should be hot linked to the table of contents matrix, with the exception of the header. They should all use the same font, the same enlarged size, and be bold.

In the calendar and content section, use catchy titles for the daily topics. "Giving thoughtful titles to each lecture is also a good idea. as we know from our own experience, we attend lectures with interesting titles and promising substantive content, so why should students in our classes act differently" (Harriet W. Sheridan Center for Teaching and Learning/Michael Woolcock ).

In some discouraging research by Smith and Razzouk in 1993, it was found that most students were unable to recall course objectives, evaluation procedures, and the discussion topic of the day (Smith and Razzouk, 1993).   For this reason, it is not only essential to prepare a professional and comprehensive near distance learning e-syllabus, but that it be effectively presented the first day and then used throughout the semester! More on this later.

It is important to know the hardware and software available to your students who will be using your e-syllabus.   Will they be using relatively slow 28.8 or 56K modems, broadband, or be part of a LAN or WAN on campus.   With the tremendous advances in computer power at reasonable costs, problems are unlikely to occur unless you use streaming video or teleconferencing/telephony links within your e-syllabus.

To provide necessary levels of internal consistency a single discipline will be highlighted in these applied steps.   However, the subject matter could have been music, anthropology, music theory or algebra. The general stages will all be very similar.  The differences will be more in the application then the process.

**Section One: The Header**

The first section of your e-syllabus should be the header.  It provides the most basic course identification material, telling the student they have arrived at the right site for this particular course and semester.  It is also valuable to the teacher in following semesters as they make revisions.  The author found it amazing the number of e-syllabi that omitted two or more of these eleven basic pieces of information. They include:

Figure 6

| | |
|---|---|
| ❖ Course title<br>❖ Department &<br>    designator<br>❖ Credit hours<br>❖ For grade or credit/no<br>    credit<br>❖ Semester<br>❖ Year<br>❖ Time and place<br>❖ Teacher's name | ❖ Program fit<br>    ➤ Free elective<br>    ➤ Business core<br>    ➤ Part of major<br>    ➤ Part of minor<br>    ➤ University required<br>    ➤ Divisional required |

> ❖ **Prerequisites**
>    ➤ Courses
>    ➤ Class standing
>    ➤ Other
> ❖ Date and time last
>    modified

These eleven pieces of information should be the first items that appear in your e-syllabus using any format that you find simple to read. The first two items should be bold and larger than the rest.

**Section Two: Flash Announcements**

Right up at the top following the header should appear a text box that contains flash announcements. These flash announcements should be urgent reminders or anything that you need to tell all your students on short notice. Students should be told during the first class period, with frequent reminders, that they need to check the flash announcements section every 48 hours.

What kinds of things might appear in this section? Maybe you are going to switch classrooms one day to facilitate a visit for a speaker or a special type of class exercise. Next week your open walk-in office hours need to be cancelled on Thursday because of a professional conference you are attending. You students have been assigned a case study that contains an error and you want them to be sure to make this correction before they compute the price/earnings ratio.

A big question is how do you get students to check these flash announcements on a regular basis. There are two ways that are sure to get their attention. The first is to announce a "surprise quiz" as a flash announcement. You can even indicate the subject matter of the quiz or the actual question if intellectually challenging. A second method is to "hide" a *treasure chest* in the flash announcement text box. This might be a piece of software available free to the students, a wonderful Internet site that will help them with their class project, or even a sign up sheet for a free dinner at your house Wednesday evening for the first 6 who discover the treasurer chest. Shrimp stir-fry of course.

The purpose of this flash announcement text box is to permit you to communicate to all your students outside of the classroom on a topic of importance. If the information is absolutely essential, you should also use your Listserv to send an email to all students. If you are using courseware such as Blackboard, this function is built into the software, usually as the second element on the first page. It allows you to highlight new announcements and retain old announcements for as many days as you wish. If you set the auto-delete at 7 days, announcements will disappear seven days after they are posted. It also allows you to give rights to post announcements to your graduate assistant if you have one.

**Section Three: Table of Contents Matrix**

The third section should be a very simple matrix with a minimum of 24 cells. Each cell should then be linked to either a subtitle or by hyperlink to the section identified in the link. This will permit easy navigation for both you and your students and make the total document appear to be well organized...because it is! The following is an example of such a table of contents matrix.

Figure 7

| Shortcut to Daily Assignments: click anywhere within this box! | | | |
|---|---|---|---|
| Flash Announce-ments | Administrative Details | Justification for Level of Detail | Teaching Philosophy |
| Mission, Values & Vision Statement | Catalogue Description | Behavioral Objectives | Communi-cations |
| Pedagogies | Faculty and Student Rights & Responsibilities | Professional Standards of Behavior | Honesty |
| Attendance | Netiquette | Grading/Assessment | B.A.R.S.* |
| Extra Credit Options* | Semester Calendar of Content | Daily Assignments (See Calendar Links) | Projects And Standards |
| Teams* | Resources and Learning Tips | Students with Disabilities or Special Circum-stances | Technical Requirements * |
| E-Suggestion Box Form | Forms, Office Hours Sign Up, Attachments, Guidelines, Acknowledg-ments | Student E-syllabus Agreement | Caveat Statement |

(Those cells marked with an asterisk may not be necessary.)

To the extent that you use this basic format with all your classes, and other faculty members adopt a similar format, students will become familiar with the navigational convenience.  Subsequent sections will continue to explain each of the cells of the matrix.

**Section Four: Administrative Details**

Section four is packed with essential information for students.  It will also contain links to optional administrative or personal details.  It is the key administrative resource page for your students.

Figure 8

```
❖   Textbook
    ➤   Title
    ➤   Authors & Publisher
    ➤   Edition Number & ISBN
    ➤   Where available
        ▪   On or off campus
        ▪   Electronic sources
            •   URLs
            •   Delivery time
            •   Shipping costs
            •   Total price
    ➤   Available new and/or used
    ➤   Date needed in class
    ➤   Resale information
    ➤   Available on library reserve?
❖   Teacher contact information
    ➤   Email address
    ➤   Office telephone number
        ▪   Hours OK
    ➤   Home telephone number
        ▪   Hours OK
    ➤   FAX number (office or home)
    ➤   Availability of voice mail
    ➤   Office location (bldg & #)
    ➤   Office hours
        ▪   Open walk-in hours
        ▪   By schedule only (explain) and link to
            Office Hours sign up form
        ▪   Special office hours before and/or after
            exams
❖   Graduate Assistant name and contact information
    if appropriate
```

Figure 8 continued

❖   Tutorial materials available and location
❖   Other important contact information
   ➢   Departmental secretary
   ➢   Departmental office boxes if ok for
      material drop off
❖   Student technology labs (people, locations,
   hours)
❖   Is audio taping OK in class?
❖   Name and number of business librarian
❖   Course withdrawal policy
   ➢   Withdrawal Fail
   ➢   Withdrawal Pass
   ➢   Withdrawal – medical

**OPTIONAL INFORMATION**
❖   Teacher: The Professional
   ➢   Teaching interests
   ➢   Degrees, areas and locations
   ➢   Other courses currently/often taught
   ➢   Research interests
   ➢   Recent publications
   ➢   Associations
   ➢   Consulting and business experience
   ➢   Professional, university, divisional,
      departmental committees
❖   Teacher: The Individual
   ➢   Family information (photos)
   ➢   Hobbies
   ➢   What you like to read
   ➢   Music preferences
   ➢   Sports interests
   ➢   Travel interests
   ➢   Pets (photos)
   ➢   Religion
   ➢   Home (photos)
   ➢   Favorite web links (URLs)
   ➢   Other
   ➢   Screen savers
❖   Other
   ➢   Favorite poet/poem
   ➢   Hobby creations
   ➢   Places you have lived
   ➢   Your High School

Depending upon the class you teach, there may be other essential administrative details you need to share. Will the students need to have access to, or purchase selected software? Is there an optional student supplement available to the text? Information related to laboratory sessions? Just put yourself in your student's shoes and think about administrative details they might want and that you are willing to share.

## Section Five: Justification for Level of Detail

Some students will be shocked by the size and complexity of your syllabus. Yours may be the first e-syllabus they have ever seen, or be considerably longer than anything they have experienced. To help them understand your motivation in developing a complete and professional e-syllabus, it is worthwhile to briefly make the following points about the reason for the detail:

1. To help the students anticipate and understand the "why's" and "what's" behind the course;
2. To avoid misunderstandings between the teacher and students;
3. As required faculty documentation for teaching portfolios, program and divisional accreditation, annual reports, and promotion and tenure;
4. As a course management tool
5. As a means of two-way communications
6. As a cognitive map of the course
7. To create a better, more flexible, interactive course
8. To teach information management

## Section Six: Teaching Philosophy

Under Step 1 in this book, a number of dimensions of your personal values, attitudes, beliefs, preferences, priorities and philosophy about teaching, learning and assessment were discussed. Having helped dozens of professors at a series of workshops to write teaching philosophy, the author has come to the conclusion that this one page document is one of the hardest things to write that you have ever attempted. To write a teaching philosophy that you really like will take many drafts over your career as a teacher. If you can talk a half dozen of your colleagues into drafting a statement of their personal teaching philosophies and then share your collective outputs, you will be astounded by all the different approaches and ideas. Borrow ideas where appropriate. Next semester do it again. In a few years you will begin to have a written teaching philosophy that truly expresses your feelings concerning teaching, learning and assessment.

## Section Seven: Course Mission, Vision and Values

In Step 5 you were challenged to write mission, vision and values statements for the courses you teach. The Mission Statement should be a universal yet meaningful expression of the courses intended operational scope, its sense of social responsibility, and its future direction. Why am I teaching this course? What do I expect my students to learn during the course? What are the most important knowledge and skill sets essential to the course? What behaviors and attitudes do I want my students to display? What one question would I like students to be able to answer at the end of this class? Look at the purpose, process and outcomes. If others teach this course, a joint effort at the mission statement would be worthwhile.

The Value Statement identifies the roles, rights and responsibilities to the stakeholders. This again should be short and macro in nature. You will have an opportunity to become more specific later in this e-syllabus. If you are completely lost, try reviewing mission, vision and value statements often published by your university, division and department. In fact, you might even consider including in this section the actual mission, vision and value statements that are published by your university, division and/or department. This will help you and your students place this particular course within a larger context.

The Vision Statement should include a general blueprint for accomplishing the organizations mission, goals and objectives. This statement will relate to process, structure and outcomes in a macro context. Review the behavioral objectives and structures discussed in Steps 7 & 9 and see if you can verbalize this vision.

All three of these statements are only second in difficulty to creating your teaching philosophy. They will take time and effort. Refinements will be needed each time you teach the course and create the e-syllabus. Eventually, you will arrive at a series of short statements, metaphors, or "other" that effectively capture the mission, values and vision of the course.

## Section Eight: Catalogue Description

This is the easiest part of your entire e-syllabus. All you need to do is either electronically reference, or retype the short course description that exists in your catalogue. Unfortunate, for many of our courses, this statement could be 10 to 20 years old, and may not represent the reality of the evolution of this course.  It is suggested that you try your hand at redrafting this statement, copy the original version with your version to the e-syllabus, and then send your description to your department chair or catalogue administrator to recommend the change.  This inclusion of a revised catalogue description in your e-syllabus will give your students due notice that things have changed and that they should rethink the course in terms of your catalogue description.

## Section Nine: Behavioral Objectives

As discussed in Step 7, behavioral objectives represent cognitive, affective and psychomotor ways of knowing, translated into a series of statements concerning what students will know, feel and be able to do by the end of the course.  How these statements are worded, and the subsequent assessment techniques selected commit the teacher to certain pedagogies, assignments, projects, processes and standards. Some of the behavioral objectives may be very specific, while others are more general or systemic in nature. Almost everything you do inside and outside the classroom and design into your e-syllabus is intended to successfully achieve these objectives.

An example behavioral objective might be "To develop your problem-solving and analytical decision-making skills in an international business environment involving risk, uncertainty and incomplete information."  A second objective might be "To refine your written and oral business communication skills, supported by modern, electronic communication technology."  These two behavioral objectives would suggest that the teacher use a variety of advanced international case studies using small groups and guided discussions and augmented by online secondary research.  The groups would be required to write up and present, using available multi-media, their recommendations with supporting evidence.  Exams would require individual or small group analysis of case studies involving a variety of international corporate situations. It might combine both written material and online corporate reports and financial information.

These behavioral learning objectives should also include common student goals such as passing a certificate or licensing exam (CPA) or improving information management skills.  Where there is significant overlap between your behavioral objectives and those of your students, you are headed for a win-win experience.  Of course, in some circumstances we will need to help students understand that our behavioral objectives for them are essential for the achievement of their behavioral objectives.  For example, how will the computation and understanding of elasticity or break even point analysis help them achieve their desire to be an entrepreneur in the automotive EOM market.

Just as important as the behavioral objectives that we include in our e-syllabus are the objectives we decide not to include.  The temptation in most of our classes is to add additional knowledge and skills without ever taking anything out of the course.  Eventually we arrive at the point where the more we teach the less they learn.  Whenever you add another behavioral objectives, review your existing objectives to see if any need to be omitted.  Of course through creative course restructuring you sometimes can do even more, particularly as you integrate knowledge and skills in unique and productive ways.

As one can see from the above, as you add additional behavioral objectives you are actually shaping the day-to-day activities and assessment methods.  Your performance as a teacher can then be judged by multiple stakeholders by one, the quality and appropriateness of your behavioral objectives to your course, and two, by the effectiveness and efficiency of the students in achieving these behavioral objectives.

Experience, unsupported by empirical research, indicates that between 5 and 12 carefully worded behavioral objectives are usually sufficient to capture both your cognitive and affective behavioral learning objectives.  Psychomotor objectives are fairly rare in the business field.  Most of our objectives are of the mind and heart and not manual dexterity, physical strength, or agility.  Of course, if one of your objectives was to help your students reduce their golf handicap by 10%, that would be different.

## Section Ten : Communications

### Email

The e-syllabus, with its IT capabilities, can be used to enhance written, oral and visual communications between teacher and student, student and teacher, student and student, teacher and teacher, and third parties with both students and teachers. "As a communication support tool, IT extends faculty availability beyond the class times and office hours, establishes student links to classmates, and enables, more efficient distribution of materials, reminders and notifications" (Benbunan-Fich and Hiltz, 1999).

Of all the new communication tools available to our students and us, the most frequently used is email.  It sometimes feels like our students expect us to be sitting at our terminal 24/7 just waiting for their email. In this dimension, the email is both a blessing and a curse. With the advent of wireless email and PDA$^s$, plus remote access from almost any computer, it is unlikely that this trend will slow. For this reason, within your communications section it is advisable to set down some guidelines for the use of email. What type of response time can your students usually expect? Will you accept class assignments as email attachments?   Do you wish to communicate certain Netiquette guidelines for student use in emails? Should you create an email list of all your students so that group members can contact each other, or is this an invasion of their privacy?   Should you set up a special topic heading standard ( Smith461C, syllabus) to readily identify your student email from other emails, or will you set up a second email account just for class traffic?

The use of email through your e-syllabus has a number of advantages for both you and your students.   As a teacher it permits increased communications with your students without playing phone tag.   You can also identify the exact time the message was sent, although a bright student can now falsify this time stamp   You can contact all your students simultaneously if something happens (like personal illness) and you need everyone to know ASAP.   You can also accept papers electronically as attachments, make constructive observations directly on the document, and then return the email to the sender.   This is particularly useful if you accept draft copies and are willing to help you students improve their business writing skills.

Lastly, email is extremely helpful when supervising independent studies or internships that take place off campus.   This allows you to stay in contact wherever you may be, therefore avoiding long periods of dead time where snail mail sits in your mailbox.

**Telephone/Telephony/Fax/Voice Mail**

The traditional telephone is also a near distance-learning tool that places you and your students in contact at a time and place other then the classroom.   While establishing rules for the use of emails, it is equally important to establish procedures for the telephone.   You may limit the use of the FAX to short documents that cannot conveniently be transmitted as attachments.   A good example would be a graduate school form for recommendations or an article from a magazine or trade journal.   Telephones can be very disruptive if you need large blocks of research time.   You may request that you only be telephoned at the office Mondays through Thursdays between 8 am and 1 pm or at home during weekdays between 7 and 8:30 pm. Voice mail can obviously be left any time, but should be short and always contain the student's telephone number and time when they can be reached.

In the coming years we will see increased use of the computer as a telephone connection in both synchronous and asynchronous modes. As this means of communications increases, particularly for inexpensive long distance learning, we will have to define parameters for its use.

**Discussion Groups**

Discussion groups, chat rooms, and electronic bulletin boards can potentially add richness to your teaching never before possible. They facilitate the exchange of ideas between students and between you and your students that can result in 100% participation, a freer flow of ideas by reluctant students (Eastman, J.K.,2001), and actually stretches the borders of your room way beyond that little block of time between 9:00 and 9:50 am on MWF. Let's start with the discussion group or groups. If you were to assign three discussions issues to the class for Thursday you won't know if and who has thought about the issues prior to your arrival at class. You won't be able to add additional material or plan a debate. What are the students thinking? Do they understand what they read? Will most of their responses fall into two or three positions? Does someone have a unique perspective on one of the issues? By posting the discussion questions on your e-syllabus in a discussion format and requiring 100% participation 24 hours prior to the class, you can direct the class period to maximize learning and sharing. Is segmentation and positioning products by racial group or religious beliefs appropriate for marketers? Read their answers, divide them into debate teams, and require them to justify their positions in class based upon marketing theory, economics and moral reasoning. The use of courseware is particularly effective for discussion groups as it permits the creation of multiple groups, the capturing of their responses, the identification of the individual "speaker," and the ability to pose additional questions if needed. Students can learn from one another before they enter the classroom. They are also learning to use IT as a idea sharing and discussion medium, a skill that will be demanded in many of their professional careers.

**Chat Rooms**

Chat rooms are a form of synchronous discussion groups requiring all participating students, and the teacher to be online at the same time. This is particularly effective for student project groups on nonresidential campuses. This permits students in separate physical locations to interact in a common "time and space" electronically. It can be used in conjunction with a discussion group by requiring the results of a chat room to be posted by a student leader (changed monthly) to report back to the class wide discussion on their findings. This also reduces the amount of reading required by the teacher if you can have a graduate assistant monitor the chat rooms.

The use of a class wide chat room is very difficult if not impossible. The lives of our students are so diverse that it is almost impossible to find a common time where everybody can participate. One possibility is to dedicate one class period every two weeks to a virtual classroom experience. If the technology exists, this can work well with outside experts who join the discussion. For example, if the topic for the day is Internet Research, what could be better then to invite an expert from Nielson to actively participate in the chat room. While she or he may not have the time to come to your campus for the day, they may be willing to spare 50 minutes as a member of the chat room. As in discussion groups, it is the teacher's responsibility to lay down guidelines related to process and netiquette in the e-syllabus.

**Electronic Bulletin Boards**

Do you have a bulletin board dedicated to the sharing of information just for your class? Can you post examples of excellent papers? Post exam grades where only the individual student can see their grade? Post maps or survey results? The electronic bulletin board provides both teachers and students the ability to have a common space just for their class where they can share information. It also allows students to read the bulletin board without actually physically coming to your office, the departmental office, or the bulletin board outside your office (The one you really don't have, or the one where things disappear). You can also use the space to post job or internship opportunities, particularly good Internet site, or again treasurer chests to encourage regular visits.

One interesting use of a bulletin board is collaborative student research on any topic. For example, if you are exploring the desirability of a particular site for a new shopping center, you could distribute in class 30-40 information questions about traffic counts, population density, location of competitors, presence of utilities, etc. Each student would be responsible for finding the answer to their questions and the posting the results. The entire class could then look at the mosaic of information and formulate an initial recommendation. A guest expert could follow this and demonstrate their software and IT GPS solutions to the questions in a more accurate and sophisticated setting. The range of use of bulletin boards is only limited by the teacher's imagination and the technology available on campus, courseware, or your Internet class page.

**Streaming Audio. Video, Teleconferencing and Animation via Phone Lines, the Internet or Satellite**

This is one area where your expertise, available technology, software and hardware, bandwidth and those of your students become key. Steaming satellite audio and video requires specialized software and hardware to receive. Teleconferencing by phone lines or the Internet also requires specialized microphones and very large screens or projection units. Animations may require software that must be purchase, downloaded, or interacts with existing systems in an unpleasant manner. Most of these have great potential as educational tools, but are well beyond most of our capabilities for another three to five years. The technology exists, but because of the cost or inconvenience, simply is not appropriate for the majority of our e-syllabus.

**Section Eleven: Pedagogies**

"Learning to think pedagogically is a sadly neglected aspect of our professional preparation as university teachers, but it is an invaluable resource for even the most retiring, yet committed teacher" (Harriet W. Sheridan Center for Teaching and Learning/Michael Woolcock). In Step 9 we discussed the breadth of instructional strategies (pedagogies, electronic media, structures) that are available to all teachers. Your choices are dictated by your behavioral objectives for the course, your teaching skills and preferences, and the nature of the audience. In this section you should describe the instructional strategies that will be used in the class and your reason for its selection. Assuming that you use multiple instructional strategies, it is helpful to the students to add the approximate percentage of the time each will be used. This section is particularly valuable to students, as they will begin to understand that the reason different classes and teachers use different instructional strategies is directly related to the behavioral learning objectives for the course. Your explanation is also useful for colleagues or administrators reading your teaching portfolio for summative or formative purposes.

**Section Twelve: Faculty and Student Rights and Responsibilities**

E-syllabi unfortunately rarely include a section that discusses the rights and responsibilities of the teacher and the students. In your experience, you have probably run into many examples of students expressing their rights, but sometimes forget their responsibilities. The students have the right to be heard, to receive the learning experiences expressed in the course behavioral objectives, to receive regular performance feedback, fairness in assessment, academic assistance during regular office hours and individual attention to the degree feasible. They, on the other hand have the responsibility to attend all classes, be prepared, actively participate in discussions, to listen and think about diverse opinions, to assist their colleagues in the learning community, to hand papers in on time, to act honestly and arrive in class on time. It is up to you to make clear to your students your expectations for their behavior. Given their diverse backgrounds, it is not realistic that they can guess or will "just know" what your expectations are for this particular course.

One option that you should consider is to request students in small groups to create a list of their and your rights and responsibilities and to share these during the first or second class period. With a little luck, the list they prepare and the list you have in mind will be very similar. The advantage of using this process is that they have developed their own list and therefore will be more likely to internalize and accept them as appropriate behaviors.

Teachers also have certain rights and responsibilities to their students. They are responsible to be on time, well prepared, current in their field, to return homework on time, encourage open dialogue and to listen to divergent viewpoints, be available during office hours, be fair and objective in assessment, and to follow published good teaching practices. They also have the right to respectful and courteous communications from students, feedback if dishonesty is discovered by students, thoughtful and objective student course evaluations, and a safe and clean classroom environment. You will probably have additional rights and responsibilities that you can add to this list.

The formal listing of these rights and responsibilities in your e-syllabus document up front the behaviors expected from both parties.

While the list will certainly not be all-inclusive, it will put the students on notice that certain behaviors are not acceptable and will not be tolerated. The lists will remind students that you as a teacher have certain rights that must be respected. It will also let your students know that you acknowledge you have certain responsibilities as a teacher and can be held accountable for these behaviors.

**Section Thirteen: Professional Standards of Behavior, Intellectual Integrity, Attendance, and Netiquette**

**Professional Standards of Behavior**

One of the reasons that students are attending your class is to become a professional within the business community. While colleges and universities are often not considered the "real world", they are the real word of academia and have the responsibility to prepare students for the real world of business. This includes helping students understand what behaviors are acceptable or not acceptable in most business environments. Some of these can be identified under student responsibilities, but can be repeated in this section for emphasis. They can relate to behavior in the classroom, during office hours, informal communication between students, or behavior during group meetings. The length of this section will depend upon your personal preferences and the level of maturity of your students. It is a particularly important section if your class contains a large number of seniors.

**Intellectual Integrity**

A good way to present this section is to start with a broad statement concerning intellectual integrity as defined in your Student Handbook, Bulletin or Honor Code. For example, Miami University's Student Handbook, Section 501 states:
"The rights and responsibilities that accompany academic freedom are at the heart of the intellectual integrity of the University. Students are therefore expected to behave honestly in their learning. Cheating and other forms of academic misconduct undermine the value of a Miami education for everyone, and especially for the person who cheats. Violations of the Academic Misconduct Policy can result in penalties ranging from grade reductions to suspension, dismissal, or expulsion from the University. Misunderstanding of the appropriate academic conduct will not be accepted as an excuse for academic misconduct. If a student is in doubt about appropriate academic conduct

in a particular situation, he or she should consult with the instructor in the course, the department chair, or the academic dean in the appropriate division so as to avoid the serious charge of academic misconduct" (Sections 501 – 507 of the Student Handbook http://www.muohio.edu/univpubs/handbook/acadregspV.html).

The sharing of the university or divisional policy informs your students that the institution has expectations concerning intellectual integrity, and that there will be costs if they choose not to follow these policies. This is a good starting point, but, in most cases, is not specific enough for your particular course. It will be helpful if you also provide answers to the following questions:

A. Can students work together on homework assignments?
B. Can a paper or project prepared for your class be used in whole, or part, in another class?
C. Is it ok to share notes with other students? Can these notes be sold?
D. Is it acceptable to use audiotapes to record classroom activities?
E. Are exams open or closed book?
F. What constitutes cheating on an exam?
G. Are past exams available for review? When and where? Under what conditions?
H. What constitutes plagiarism? How should quotations or paraphrased material be acknowledged?

If procedures for the handling of cases of dishonesty are electronically available, the site should be identified. This also should be done for possible disciplinary actions and the grievance procedure that is available to the student.

The final part of this section should contain a simple statement that you will follow the mandated procedures and policies of the university, division and department and that they should not risk their academic career or personal integrity by being dishonest.

**Attendance**

Attendance policies vary from college-to-college, division-to-division, department-to-department, and even class-to-class. This is a dimension of class that can take an inordinate amount of your time as a teacher. To reduce or eliminate misunderstandings and reduce headaches, you should very clearly spell out your attendance policy and the reason behind that policy. If you policy is that attendance is totally up to the student, state that clearly up front. On the other hand, if attendance is required and penalties exist for missing classes, these should be made clear. The following issues should be addressed for your students:

❖ Acknowledge that they have a demanding schedule with classes, works, friends, and family
❖ Explain the cost of missing classes (estimated cost per class, need for their participation in class, the valuable information they will be missing, the opportunity for them to develop listening and speaking skills in class)
❖ Indicate any other reasons you have instituted the attendance policies
❖ How will attendance be taken?
❖ What is he maximum number of absences allowed?
❖ If you come late to class, are you considered absent?
❖ What constitutes an excused absence?
❖ What is your policy on excused absences, such as required documentation and time limits?
❖ Need for prior notification for non-emergency excused absences?
❖ What is your policy concerning absences resulting in missed quizzes and exams?
❖ What are the penalties for being absent? (Be very specific.)

If the students are clearly informed of your policies and the consequences of violating these policies, there will be fewer headaches throughout the semester.

It is also recommended that you establish a very easy process for checking for absences that is appropriate to the size and physical setting of your class. You may find it convenient for classes under 45 to have a daily attendance sign up sheet at a table near the entrance to the room. Any special handouts needed for that day or old papers being returned are also at the table. Students are asked to sign in and pick up assignments or graded papers (grades always on the back) as they enter the room. They are also informed that signing someone else's name is an act of dishonestly and will result in dismissal from the course.

## Netiquette

This part of section twelve may not be necessary for your class if you make limited use of interactive synchronous or asynchronous communication technologies, but is worthwhile for your students as future business professionals. The easiest way to accomplish this task is to request that your students go to the site www.albion.cm/netiquette/ and follow the guidelines contained therein. This site contains the core rules of netiquette, a summary of the key points in the book <u>Netiquette</u>, and a netiquette quiz to test your knowledge. If you are also using chat rooms or discussion groups, you may wish to establish some basic guidelines for your students (Palloff and Pratt, 1999).

**Section Fourteen: Assessment, BARS and Extra Credit Options**

Unfortunately, in the minds of your students, this may be one of the most important sections of your e-syllabus. Students often appear to be more interested in the grade they have been "given" than the level of learning that is reflected by the grade. For the new and inexperienced teacher, grading is probably the most frustrating and negative dimension of the entire teaching experience. Even for the experienced teacher, the process of assessment rarely is one of the favorite aspects of teaching.

All assessment tools, whether projects, papers, multiple choice, true/false, essay, short answer or other, should reflect the behavioral objectives of the course and the level of knowing specified in those objectives.

"According to Angelo and Cross 1993, assessment should be focused on improving learning, directed by the teacher for his or her teaching style and beneficial to both students and teachers. Techniques should be chosen that match the particular needs of the students and teacher, and the process should be ongoing" (Benbunan-Fich, 2001). The weighting of assessment tools is also important. "Another point to bear in mind is that the weighting you allocate to each item of assessment should reflect its importance as stated in your course objectives" (Harriet. W. Sheridan Center for Teaching and Learning/Michael Woolcock).

Students differ in their abilities to demonstrate accurately their levels of knowledge and skills, therefore making a diversity of assessment methods desirable to achieve convergent validity and objective confidence in the outcomes. "A combination of qualitatively different types of assessment procedures is needed to assess course objectives effectively [relates to learning styles]. It is also important to regard these different assessment procedures as complementary, and themselves capable of serving as teaching instruments. Try to tap into as many different avenues of student learning as possible. Some students speak well in section, for example, but don't perform well on exams; others do very well on multiple-choice exams without doing a lot of serious work" (Harriet W. Sheridan Center for Teaching and Learning/Michael Woolcock ). Michael Woolcock also suggests that you collect some shorter papers early in the semester so that feedback can be given. This will result in better major papers later when they are submitted for grades.

After indicating to your students the types of assessment tools to be used in the class, the rationale behind using these tools, and the relative weight of each assessment tool, the students will need to know answers to the following questions:

- What are the grade ranges or number of points needed to achieve specific grades?   -
- Do you curve any of the assessment tools?
- Are students in competition with one another or against absolute standards established by the teacher?
- What are the due dates of the exams and projects/papers?
- Over the past couple of years, what was the average GPA in this class? Approximate distribution of grades?
- If optional at your college or university, do you use plus/minus grading?
- When and how will you inform students of their grades to date? Electronically?
- Will you be grading all student materials, or will a graduate assistant be involved in the process?
- Do you have a grade grievance procedure? Specifics? Timing? Process? Might the grade go up or down if/when reviewed?
- Have you provided examples of past exams, papers and/or projects in the appendix of this e-syllabus?
- Are in-class exams open-book and notes or closed book?
- For large sections, will picture ID$^s$ be required to take the exam?
- Is there a standardized departmental final exam for this course?
- Guidelines for grading projects?
- If a student misses an exam, what procedures if any, exist for a make up exam?
- Statement that exams belong to the teacher and the answers/papers/projects belong to the students. The unauthorized removal of an exam will be considered an act of dishonesty and will result in an "F" for the (exam or course).
- The availability of review sessions or tutors?
- If peer review grades are to be used in group projects, explain the process;
- If you use individual learning contracts, explain.
- Verbally describe what you mean by the grades A, B, C, D and F.
- Is attendance factored into grades, and if so, how?

❖ Since regular attendance at all classes is an expectation of most colleges and universities, you are encouraged to think carefully before offering incentive grades for attendance.

❖ Make assessment tools learning opportunities. Review the outcomes with the students. If you have written a bad question, admit it and alter the grades; however, don't let students cajole you into accepting a wrong answer because.. ) If it is wrong, it is wrong!  This is not a popularity contest.

❖ Consider opportunities for self-assessment prior to major exams or the submission of written projects.

❖ What is your policy on the posting of grades (must be consistent with university regulations)?  Some courseware will allow you to post student grades with only that student having access to his or her grade.

❖ If you use participation grades, how do you come up with these grades?  Aren't they arbitrary and subjective?  (More on this under BARS.)

Finally, never apologize for grades.  If you do the best you can to objectively measure the level of achievement of your students against your behavioral objectives, that is all that can be asked. If executed conscientiously and professionally, you are only recording student outputs and then translating these into numbers and letters that represent their level of achievement.  Students give themselves grades. You design the system and are "just" the recorder.

**Behaviorally Anchored Rating Scales (BARS)**

BARS represent a method by which objectivity and consistency can be improved in the recording of participation grades. They also help students understand what they have to do to receive good participation grades and the difference between the quantity and quality of "verbiage" displayed in class.

The process of creating a BARS scale takes about 20 minutes of class time and another 45 minutes of your time.  In class, ask the students to get into small groups and to write down observable behaviors that occur during a discussion that represent excellent, very good, average, poor or very poor contributions to the achievement of defined class behavioral objectives.  For example, if a student repeats a point just made, this contributes nothing to the discussion, indicates that the student was not an active listener, and would be judged as a "very poor" contribution.  On the other hand, a student who shares a unique and overlooked fact, process or observation that moves the discussion forward for everyone would be judged excellent.  The repeating of a fact, converted into useful information might be a very good contribution.    The fact alone without interpretation and implications might be rated somewhere between average and poor.

Ask each group to submit their lists to you. Before the next class, sort out 4-5 statements that you agree describe behavior at each of the five levels (excellent = A; B = very good, etc.). Add your own descriptive statements. Create a chart on your e-syllabus that contains this information and share it with your students at the next class period. This then becomes your model for judging daily individual contributions.   The smaller the class, the easier it is to remember the contributions to discussion of each student. If you have the luxury of a graduate student present in the classroom, they can be extremely helpful in capturing this information.   Otherwise, it is up to you to know your students, remember the nature and level of their contributions, and to record as soon as possible after class their participation grade for the day. If they are not present, obviously their contribution grade for that day is "very poor" and should be so reflected. You may decide to drop the two worst participation grades at the end of the semester allowing for any student to have a couple of "bad days".  A non-grade can be recorded for an excused absence.

**Extra Credit Options**

One decision teachers constantly face is the availability of extra credit projects to allow students to improve their grade for the class. This is a very individual faculty decision requiring a lot of thought by the professor. These tend to take a lot of time to supervise and grade. If made available to any one student, they must be made available to every student in the class. An even playing field is required both out of fairness, equity and often within published good teaching practices. If you decide to offer an extra credit option, the information concerning its nature, availability and magnitude of the extra credit should be indicated here.   There should then be a hot link to the details of the extra credit project.

**Section Fifteen: Calendars and Content/Daily Assignment Details (DAD)**

It is now time to indicate to the students the knowledge and skills learning modules that will be taught on a day-to-day basis. This should be set up as a calendar of dates and topics with both fun and informative titles.  Each class day in the calendar is then hot linked to the details of the actual learning module.   For example, your first month calendar might look like the follow for a *Principles of Marketing* Class:

| August 25<sup>th</sup> & 27<sup>th</sup> What is this course all about? Marketing: The big picture Click here | Sept. 1<sup>st</sup> & 3<sup>rd</sup> How does a marketer develop relationships through customer focus? Are marketer's ethical? Click here | Sept. 7<sup>th</sup> & 8<sup>th</sup> Customer service and satisfaction. The marketing environment. Click here | Sept. 10<sup>th</sup> & 13<sup>th</sup> Global dimension of marketing. Starbucks in Japan. Click here |
|---|---|---|---|
| READY | READY | READY | READY |
| Sept. 15<sup>th</sup> & 17th Strategic planning and forecasting. Will Kimberly wet toilet paper really sell? Click here  READY | Sept. 20th Marketing Research: A prologue to knowing and doing. Click here | Sept. 22<sup>nd</sup> Decision Support Systems and IT The computer and ERP (excuse me) to the rescue. Click here | Sept. 24<sup>th</sup> Exam #1 What do I know and am able to do so far? Click here |

This calendar gives a student a quick overview of the topic for the day, what's happening for the coming week, and where to go for the specifics.   Each cell should represent a unit of learning derived from your behavioral objectives. Each cell is then linked electronically to another page that provides the details concerning that module. Both the "click here" and the image should be created as hotlinks. This calendar should also include key dates of interest to the student, such as: last day to file for graduation, university holidays, special events on campus related to your discipline, etc.

You are probably ready at the beginning of the semester to lay out the topics for all the months of the semester, but have not prepared the individual DAD[5] activities in detail. You should inform the students that when the word **READY** appears in the cell in red, that the learning module is ready for them to start working on as time permits. Students are not going to be working weeks in advance. As long as you stay a couple of weeks ahead, you will be in good shape. This also allows you to alter the content or exercises as you discover new materials or experience gaps in student knowledge and skills that need additional work.

**Section Sixteen: Daily Assignments Linked to the Calendar**

This section will actually consist of a separate electronic page for each day of class. The layout of this page should be consistent so that students become comfortable with its' format. The page should normally include the following:

❖ Date
❖ Subject matter
❖ Relevant behavioral objective for this learning module: "know and be able to do"
❖ Preparation needed prior to the class including assigned exercises to be completed, discussion questions, issues to consider, information to discover, and other
❖ Assignments for discussion groups, chat rooms, bulletin boards, etc.
❖ Electronic resources to be used (URLs, digitized articles, pictures, tables, sound files, videos, excel spreadsheets, PowerPoint files, Word files, etc.)
❖ Non electronic media; read Chapter "X" in our textbook
❖ Instructional strategies for the module
❖ Material to download and have available in class (charts, diagrams, cases, partial class notes outline, other)

As explained in section fifteen, these individual class period learning modules can be refined and updated as your semester progresses. Very few of us are so organized that they would have ALL the details of the daily assignments finalized prior to the beginning of the semester. An example learning module might look like the following:

**Date:** October 4, 2002

**Subject matter:**
Strategic planning;
New product introductions;
Identifying corporate strengths, weaknesses, opportunities & threats;
Creation of a corporate mission, value and vision statement
Identification and analysis of corporate goals from secondary sources;
Identification and analysis of corporate objectives from secondary sources;

**Behavioral objectives:**
Using pubic secondary information, identify and critically analyze Kimberly-Clark's goals (quantitative) and objectives (qualitative) for the corporation, and more specifically the Tissue division;
Formulate a mission, value and vision statement based upon your interpretation of these goals and objectives for Kimberly – Clark, and more specifically their Tissue Division;
Based upon the mission, value, vision, goals and objectives, does the proposed new Cottenelle Fresh™ Rollwipes toilet paper represent a "good" (i.e. potentially profitable) product line extension?

**Preparation before class:**
List at least 15 objectives of Kimberly–Clark (to be typed and handed in at the end of class)
List at least 20 goals of Kimberly-Clark (to be typed and handed in at the end of class)
Create and print using PowerPoint a one page, three level divisional organization chart for Kimberly-Clark (to be collected at the end of the class)
Read "Toilet-Paper War Heats Up With New, Wet Roll", WSJ, 11/17/01

    1.   Carefully read the following four web sites and related links in order to be able to answer parts one, two and three: www.kimberlyclark.com
http://www.rollwipes.com/
www.kimberlyclark.com/index
www.newscom.com/cgi-bin/prnh/soo1o116/datuoo4-a

**Postings:**
Go to your favorite electronic financial resource and find out what analysts are saying about Kimberly-Clark.  Post your findings on the

course bulletin board by noon on October 3$^{rd}$; one paragraph only please

**Other electronic sources:**   None

**Non-electronic media:**
Kimberly-Clark Annual Report 2001 is available in King Library
Reading Room, First floor **(optional reading)**

**Instructional strategies:**
      We will break up into five to eight groups to create master lists of goals, objectives and a single mission, value and vision statement per table.  These will be written on our white boards and presented to the rest of the class.(45 minutes).
      We will collectively discuss the viability of Cottenelle Fresh$^{TM}$ Rollwipes as a viable line extension and for fit with corporate goals and objectives (20 minutes)
      During the last five minutes, each student will be asked to write on a 5 x 8 card if the think Kimberly-Clark should proceed with this roll and the three most important facts that support your position. (5 minutes) - graded

**Bring to class:**
List of at least 15 objectives of Kimberly–Clark (to be typed and handed in at the end of class) - graded
List of at least 20 goals of Kimberly-Clark (to be typed and handed in at the end of class) - graded
Create and print using PowerPoint a one page, three level divisional organization chart for Kimberly-Clark (to be collected at the end of the class) - graded
Other notes you have taken while viewing the websites
**The above can be the combined work of two people.**

**Section Seventeen: Projects, Standards, Guidelines, and Suggested Tmelines**

      In the majority of courses taught in Departments of Marketing or Schools of Business Administration, one or more projects are build into the instructional strategies.  Students as individuals or in teams execute these projects.  They can be as short as a one page reflective paper, or very comprehensive, full semester research projects.  Whatever the nature of the project, it is essential to provide your students with enough information to perform well.  The types of information that should be included about each course project are:

❖ The behavioral objectives of the project
❖ To be done individually or in teams?
❖ If group: how many in the group, selection process, desired talent mix, constraints, rules for conflict resolution, can a team "fire" a member, team assessment process
❖ Time line: start, stages and due time/date
❖ How will the project be graded?
❖ Format and technical requirements
❖ Available guidelines for written and oral format
❖ Availability of past projects available for review as an electronic attachment to your e-syllabus
❖ Penalties if late
❖ Suggested do's and don'ts

**Section Eighteen: Teams in the Classroom or on Projects**

Some of your students may have taken a course that includes instruction on team building processes, while others have not.  Teams are widely used in business and therefore provide the opportunity for students to develop skills that will be needed.  They are also a useful means for teachers to reduce their grading workloads for large classes. If done well, they can be outstanding opportunities for peer teaching and learning and the acquisition of small group communication skills. They can also be disasters!  How many times have we heard that certain members of the team are not contributing and "it's just not fair"?  For this reason it is important to consider providing the class with some fundamental insights concerning team dynamics and leadership, or at a minimum a complete set of guidelines and outside references they can go to for help.  The decisions you will need to make include:

❖ Will the teacher form the groups, and if so, on what basis?
❖ If you permit the students to form their own teams, what do you do about the "orphans"?
❖ What is the optimal size for the group, given the behavioral objectives of the project?
❖ Who will select the team leader?
❖ Do you have the ability to create an electronic bulletin board, chat room and/or discussion group to facilitate remote interaction?

❖Should you schedule a series of regular meetings with the groups on major projects?
❖Required format of team output?
❖Will you require the team members to maintain work logs?
❖What standards will be used to grade the team project?
❖Under what conditions can a team fire a member of the team? Process? Alternatives open to a member that has been fired?
❖Will peer reviews be used? Process? How will this input become part of the grading process?
❖Will your teams be composed of members from a single class? Multiple sections of the same class? Different classes within your department or division? Across universities or even international boundaries?

If your class will not require teams either inside or outside of class, this section can be omitted.

**Section Nineteen: Learning Resources and Tips**

One of the significant advantages of an e-syllabus is the ability to make multiple resources available online, either as attachments, embedded media, or links to Internet or digital files. If you have a number of articles or current events that you wish to include in your course, have them scanned into a digital format and then allow your students to read them either online, or to download them if they refer. Hot links to Internet sites can be created to support daily learning modules. If you believe in providing your students with class notes (frameworks only or full notes), they can be placed here or on your daily assignment pages.

Some faculty members use this section to provide links to professional associations, professional literature, and supplemental lecture materials. Audio and video files can be hot linked. This section can also contain information that will be useful to students in communicating among themselves. A directory of students and their email and telephone numbers (with their permission) can be included. This would be a good place to store past projects for easy access. If you so desire, they can be placed in a read only format if you prefer that the students not be able to download hardcopies.

This would be an appropriate place to provide "hints on how to best learn in this course". You can provide the types of suggestions that are particularly appropriate for achieving your behavioral objectives, given your learning strategies and methods of student assessment. For example, the types of suggestions might include:

❖ Do homework at least 48 hours before class to let the ideas sink in.
❖ Highlight important ideas in your textbook; then create an outline of important ideas.  If done well, you should not need to review or reread your textbook before exams.
❖ Try to answer the discussion questions at the end of each chapter? They are a good source for exam questions for the teacher.
❖ Take structured notes in your own words in class.  Compare the notes with a friend's and add to them as necessary.
❖ Always try to think of business applications of the theories and concepts covered in class.  Application skills are important.
❖ Study in groups, but be sure the giving and receiving is balanced
❖ Don't resort to cramming right before exams.  This results in short term learning and retention of knowledge. Learn for life and your profession, not just to pass the exam.
❖ Study in a manner consistent with the format of the exam. You need to study very differently for a multiple-choice exam in comparison to an essay exam.

## Section Twenty: Students with Disabilities and Special Circumstances

It is essential that teachers provide reasonable accommodations for students with documented learning disabilities or special needs both as a matter of conscious and also as a matter of law.   These accommodations may take the form of special seating arrangements, the use of audio recorders, or special conditions for the giving and taking of examinations.  In this section you should request that students with documented learning disabilities, special needs, religious requirements, or approved activities that will result in missing classes (like varsity athletes) inform you in writing, with documentation of the existing circumstances during the first week of class.   Individual meetings with the students can then be arranged to discuss the specific actions that will be taken.   The intended outcomes of these accommodations should be the provision of an equitable and "level as possible playing field" for all your students.

One special circumstance that often provides unique challenges for teachers is student absences from class due to personal or family emergencies, illness, religious holidays, or university functions.  Your first step is to determine if university regulations exist that cover these circumstances.   For example, some colleges and universities now publish a list of religious holidays that fall on school days and that forbid the student from attending class. The university may also publish a list of "approved" university functions and suggested/required accommodations that can be made available for those students. Illness or personal tragedies are a much more difficult situation because of the difficulty or awkwardness of documentation and variations possible. The important thing is that you write in this section a policy that you can implement consistently, fairly and humanely, while protecting the academic integrity of your course.

**Section Twenty-one: Technical Class Requirements**

In some business classes, you may have technical requirements that must be followed by all students enrolled in this course. For the use of an e-syllabus, the students must have computer access to your site. If you are using specific courseware, it is usually required that they log in and provide certain information to become part of the electronic community. If you have decided to use certain types of print or multi-media files, you may require them to download a PDF Reader or Quick Time and RealPlayer Basic software off the web. If you are concerned about email contamination due to a variety of viruses, you can require certain minimal VirusScan software. If the students will be submitting materials on a disc, you may require that the disc be new and only contain files for your course.

Besides hardware and software, you course may require proof of certain technical skills. At Miami University, five computer exams must be mastered prior to taking a sophomore level or above business class. If your course require a minimal technical computer competency, you could require your students to have 1) taken satisfactorily a certain course; 2) passed a technology proficiency exam, or 3) to take a self-paced test on your homepage or courseware with a grade of 70% or better.

**Section Twenty-two: The E-Suggestion Box**

It is suggested that you create an electronic form for students to use to provide anonymous or signed suggestions any time during the semester. This form should contain a suggestion form of "I like…" and "I wish…" so that students are encouraged to provide both positive and constructive ideas. Under the "I wish…" section, a subsection should request the student's recommendation on how their suggestion can be best implemented and why it will result in a more productive learning environment.

Students should be encouraged to deliver this form to you personally, to your mailbox anonymously, or as an attachment to an email. These e-suggestions are most helpful to you if the sender is identified as you can go to that student for clarification and further information as needed.

If your students are reluctant to use these e-suggestions, you can require that all students submit a signed or unsigned form on the fifth and tenth week of the semester. Inform the students that you will carefully read all their suggestions and respond to them in class. Suggestions that will improve the learning climate of the class and result in better achievement your learning objectives will be initiated immediately. Those suggestions that you believe would not have these results should also be addressed with appropriate explanations.

This section would also be a good place to explain the student evaluation forms used by most universities at the close of the semester. Most students have no idea if or how their input is used and the impact their comments have upon the faculty. Without influencing the process in a bias manner, a straightforward description of the form and how it is used, combined with the fact that it should be taken seriously and completed with care should be included.

**Section Twenty-three: Forms, Student Information Sheets, Acknowledgments, and "Have Read" Forms**

This section should include any forms that the students will need for your course, plus student information sheets, "have read" forms, and your personal acknowledgements related to resources or individuals that have aided you in the writing or technical aspects of your e-syllabus.

First, what types of forms might your consider. If your students are being asked to critique articles or web sites on a regular basis, it may be helpful to provide them with a basic form that can be completed and submitted. Another form could be a peer evaluation form to be used for their team projects. A third form might be a standardized format for the posting of certain types of messages on the course bulletin board.

A second type of form that is highly recommended is a "have read" form. This is a very simple statement that " I, _____, have completely read this e-syllabus and understand and agree to comply with the course requirements. Date: _____. Signature: _____" (paraphrased Garavalia, L.S., 1999). This completed form should be required as the students enter the second or third class of the semester. This commits the students to the written policies of your e-syllabus and encourages them to carefully read the entire document prior to signing the document. If a student fails to submit this document, you will need to decide on how to handle the situation. Do they not understand parts of your e-syllabus or are they refusing to comply with the requirements of the course. In the first case, this provides you with the opportunity to further explain the provisions they do not understand, and potentially add clarification to your e-syllabus. If they are unwilling to comply with the conditions for the course, you may suggest that they should explore some other section or course.

A third document that is highly recommended is a student information sheet. This will help you get to know your students, communicate to them directly when necessary, and to better customize the course to their current level of learning and personal and professional needs. Students have the right to leave some sections blank if they feel it is invasion of their privacy; however this only happens in less than one out of a hundred cases. The information that should be gathered on the form includes:

❖ Full name
❖ Name they wish to be called in class
❖ Major and minor
❖ Credit hours completed to date
❖ University address
❖ Home address
❖ Current telephone number and email address
❖ Photo attachment
❖ Job experience to date (dates, positions, companies)
❖ Business experience of immediate family members
❖ If a medical condition exists that could become critical during class, a medical emergency contact person and telephone number
❖ Interviewing intentions if appropriate
❖ "Two things that make you unique"
❖ Birthday – date and year
❖ Other information that would be of assistance in customizing your course.

In any class under 45-50, the personal information sheets can be extremely useful to get to know your students and to put together names and faces. The photos will be very helpful during the early weeks of the semester if you use participation grading in your classroom. Provisions should be made for the digital taking or scanning of students' pictures by your IT personnel. You can also take the pictures on the first day of class with a digital camera, download the pictures to your e-syllabus, and then have the students take their picture form the general file and transfer it to the student information sheet. These pictures also prevent a "stand in" student from taking one of your exams.

Knowing the students' and parents' business backgrounds permits you to tap into this information during discussions to the benefit of all the students. Family members may be excellent potential class speakers. The birthday information can be used to schedule a Happy Birthday card from Hallmark or Blue Mountain web sites on these special days. Particularly informative are the comments students add concerning what makes them particularly unique. This may provide the teacher with a real insight into the person and something the student considers important. On the other hand you sometimes learn more then you want to know!

The least part of this section could contain an acknowledgement to persons or resources that have been helpful in preparing or implementing this e-syllabus. This could include mentors, colleagues or speakers who will assist with the class.

## Section Twenty-four: Caveat Boilerplate Statement

No matter how carefully you have prepared this starting draft of your e-syllabus, situations will come up to that necessitate changes. If fact, one of the major reasons you have created an e-syllabus instead of a traditional, handout-at-the-beginning written syllabus, is that you will be able to make additions and deletions throughout the course. To protect your right to make these changes, it is a good idea to add the following final statement to your syllabus.

*I reserve the right to make alterations to this e-syllabus at any time if I believe that they will assist the class in more effectively or efficiently achieving the mission, vision, value, or behavioral objectives of the course. All changes will be posted on the e-syllabus, announced in class, or both. It is your responsibility to be aware of these changes posted or announced within 48 hours of being posted. All changes will be in the color orange.*

**PART FOUR**
**INTRODUCING THE SYLLABUS INTO THE CLASSROOM**

The creation of the e-syllabus is an important process for you as it forces you to follow a logical and comprehensive model. However, even the most fantastic e-syllabus will not reach its potential unless it becomes an interactive communication medium between you and your students and between and among your students.

The first step in hooking your students on the e-syllabus is not to provide a hard copy of the e-syllabus to your students. This is easy to say, but considerably more difficult to implement. To do this, you will need to conduct the first day of class in a teaching computer lab where all the students, either individually or in pairs, have access to computers and software to reach your e-syllabus. If you are using courseware you will need each student to log in and enter a password to secure access. The alternative is to use a technology room that has computer projection equipment or can handle mobile computer/projection systems. IF you have a means of communicating to your students prior to the first day, such as through your books store or the Registrar's Listserv, you could request them to visit the site of your e-syllabus before the first day and to come prepared with questions.

The first third of the first class the students should be asked to surf your sight, discover what it contains, and make a list of questions not answered by the e-syllabus. If you have decided to take the student's pictures in class with a digital camera, this can be done during this time. You can then post the pictures in your e-syllabus and have the students cut and paste them into their Personal Information Sheets. The second third of the class should be devoted to answering these student's questions. If they only have a few questions, you can direct them to specific sections, such as flash announcements, the calendar or the daily schedule for the second day in class. This is a good time to point out that for the second day they must present a signed hard copy of the "Have Read..." and the "Personal Information Sheet". You can also review the basic components of the calendar and daily schedule pages to point out the common format that will be used during the class.   If you have decided to use B.A.R.S., this might be a good time to break them into small groups to prepare the descriptive behavioral responses. If time is tight, you can convert this into an assignment for each student to bring to the second class period.

It is important to point out all the multi-media functions that you are using such as chat rooms, discussion groups and the bulletin board. A comment concerning the regular visitation of the site, the flash announcements, and the occasional treasurer chests that will be placed in the e-syllabus would be appropriate.   If you have color-coded different elements of the e-syllabus, explain that blue is a hot link, red is a ready Daily Assignment Description, etc.

From this point on, it is important to either use in class or refer to the e-syllabus on a regular basis.  Most of your students will not yet be accustomed to daily use of this electronic media.

You are on your own.  You should feel free to customize your e-syllabus wherever desirable. Add new suggestions and subtract others. Remain flexible…and have fun.

Good luck!!!

## APPENDIX A

### E-SYLLABI VISITED AND BIBLIOGRAPHY

#### E-SYLLABI VISITED

1. Agarwal, Rajshree. University of Central Florida, *Using the Internet for Business* (GEB 3930), Fall 1998.
2. Balsley, Ronald D. Idaho State University, *Marketing on the Internet* (BA 446), Spring 1998.
3. Barr, Terri Feldman. Miami University, *Sales Management* (MKT 401), Spring 2001.
4. Beaty, Francine. Miami University, *Principles of Marketing* (MKT 291), Spring 2001.
5. Bennett, John F. Stephens College, *Marketing on the Internet* (BUS 345), 1998.
6. Bennett, John F. Stephens College, *Marketing on the Internet*, Spring 2001.
7. Berger, Karen and Meyer, Jeanine. Pace University, *Internet Marketing* (MAR 396), 1998/1999.
8. Berger, Karen and Meyer, Jeanine. Pace University, *Strategic Internet Marketing* (MAR 349), Summer 2000.
9. Boyd, Thomas. Miami University, *Buyer Behavior* (MKT 391), Spring 2001.
10. Boyd, Thomas. Miami University, *Sport Marketing* (MKT 485), Spring 2001.
11. Brandabur, Tim. Miami University, *Principles of Marketing* (MKT 291), Spring 2001.
12. Brown, Alex. University of Delaware, *Marketing and Electronic Commerce* (BUAD 884), Summer 2000.
13. Bruner II, Gordon C. Southern Illinois University, *Consumer Behavior*, Summer 2000.
14. Burke, Jim and McNally, Randall. Santa Rosa Junior College, *Doing Business on the Internet*, 1998/1999.
15. Chakraborty, Goutam. Oklahoma State University, *Electronic Commerce and Interactive Marketing* (MKTG 4433), Summer 1998.
16. Cole, Carolyn. University of Iowa, *Introduction to Marketing* (6M: 100), Fall 1999.
17. Cox, Janice. Miami University, *Principles of Marketing* (MKT 291), Spring 2001.

18. Di Benedetto, Anthony. Temple University, *Marketing Strategy* (MKT 506), Fall 1999.
19. Drea, John T. Western Illinois University, *Marketing Principles* (MKTG 327), Fall 1998.
20. Drea, John T. Western Illinois University, *Consumer Behavior*, Spring 1999.
21. Ekin, Cemal A. Providence University, *The Art and Science of Marketing Research* (MKT 434), Fall 1998.
22. Ekin, Cemal A. Providence University, *Marketing on the Internet*, Winter 1999.
23. Ekin, Cemal A. Providence University, *Marketing Strategy*, Spring 2001.
24. Elam, Michael. Miami University, *Principles of Marketing* (MKT 291), Spring 2001.
25. Eppright, David R. University of West Florida, *Marketing on the Internet* (MAR 5726), 1998.
26. Galletta, Dennis. University of Pittsburgh, *Commerce on the Information Highway '99* (BA MIS 2578), Spring 1999.
27. Galletta, Dennis. University of Pittsburgh, *Electronic Commerce*, Summer 2000.
28. Gifford, John B. Miami University, *Marketing Strategy* (MKT 491), Spring 2001
29. Graeff, Marcia L. Miami University, *Principles of Marketing* (MKT 291), Spring 2001.
30. Greenlee, Tim. Miami University, *Marketing Analysis* (MKT 351), Spring 2001.
31. Hansen, Randall S. Stetson University, *Special Topics. Internet Marketing* (MKT 445), Summer 1998.
32. Herbig, Paul. Tri-State University, *Marketing Research*, Fall 1999.
33. Herbig, Paul. Tri-State University, *Principles of Marketing* (MKT 303), Fall 1999.
34. Hofacker, Charles. The Florida State University, *Marketing on the Internet* (RBA 106), Spring 1999.
35. Hofacker, Charles. The Florida State University, *Marketing Research* (MAR 613), Spring 2000.
36. Hoffman, Donna L. Vanderbilt University, *Marketing in Computer-Mediated Environments* (Management 565A), Fall 1997.
37. Hyman, Michael. New Mexico State University, *Marketing Research*, Fall 1998.
38. Hyman, Michael. New Mexico State University, *Applied Marketing Research*, Fall 1999.

39. Johlke, Mark C. University of North Carolina at Willingham, *Retail Management* (MKT 346), Summer 1998.
40. Johlke, Mark C. University of North Carolina at Willingham, *Principles of Marketing* (MKT 340), Fall 1998.
41. June, Jeffrey. Miami University, *Financial Aspects of Entrepreneurial Ventures* (FIN 306), Spring 2001.
42. Kent, Bob and Brown, Alex. University of Delaware, *Marketing and Electronic Commerce*, Spring 1998.
43. Klein, Lisa R. Harvard Extension School, *Doing Business on the Internet* (CSS 103), Fall 1998.
44. Klopfenstein, Bruce C. Bowling Green State University, *New Electronic Media: The Internet and World Wide Web*, Fall 1998.
45. Kohli, Rajeev. Columbia University, *Information Technology*, 1999.
46. Langford, Barry E. Florida Gulf Course University, *Marketing on the Internet*, Summer 1998.
47. Lesser, Jack. Miami University, *Marketing Research* (MKT 451), Spring 2001.
48. Levine, Mark. California State University – Chico, *Understanding Global Business*, UNKNOWN
49. Liu, Fang. The University of Western Australia, *Promotional Strategy* (238), Winter 2001.
50. McBride, Mark. Miami University, *Economics of the Internet*, Spring 1999.
51. McCann, John M. Duke University, *Marketing and Technology* (BA 491.33), 1998.
52. McCarthy, Michael S. Miami University, *Promotion Strategy* (MKT 441), Spring 2001.
53. McNeilly, Kevin. Miami University, *International Business* (MGT/MKT 371), Spring 1999.
54. McNeilly, Kevin. Miami University, *Professional Services Marketing* (MKT 611), Spring 2001.
55. Miller, Fred. Murray State University, *Information Management in Technology* (MKT575), Spring 1999.
56. Miller, Fred. Murray State University, *Marketing Applications in eBusiness*, Spring 2001.
57. Mohr, Jakki. The University of Montana – Missoula, *Marketing of High Technology Products and Innovations*, Fall 1999.
58. Morris, Michael. Miami University, *Guerrilla Marketing* (MKT 311), Spring 2001.
59. Morris, Michael H. Miami University, *Entrepreneurship: Theory & Practice* (MKT 691), Spring 2001.

60. Oakenfull, Gillian. Miami University, *International Marketing* (MKT 471), Spring 2001.
61. Oliva, Terence A. Temple University, *Principles of Marketing*, Fall 2000.
62. Oliva, Terence A. Temple University, *Marketing Strategy* (W360), Spring 2001.
63. Ownbey, James S. Oklahoma State University, *Principles of Marketing* (MKT 3213), Fall 1998.
64. Ownbey, James S. Oklahoma State University, *Sales Management* (MKTG 3513), Fall 2000.
65. Perner, Lars. University of Maryland, *Consumer Analysis*, Spring 1999.
66. Perner, Lars. George Washington University, *International Marketing* (IBUS 166), Fall 2000.
67. Pope, Nigel. Griffith University, *Interactive Marketing* (MKT7008), 1999.
68. Rangaswamy, Arvind. Penn State University, *Ecommerce* (MKT597), 2001.
69. Roldan, Malu. Berkeley, *Network Commerce* (BA 248), Fall 1997.
70. Rosenthal, David. Miami University, *Marketing Strategy* (MKT 491), Spring 2001.
71. Schaffer, Robert W. California State University – Pomona, *Marketing on the Internet* (IBM 403), Spring 1998.
72. Schindehutte, Minet. Miami University, *Entrepreneurship New Ventures* (BUS 467), Spring 2001.
73. Schindehutte, Minet. Miami University, *Product Planning, Innovation and Technology* (MKT 481), Spring 2001.
74. Sinha, Jay. Temple University, *Marketing Research*, Spring 1998.
75. Sinha, Jay. Temple University, *Product Management* (MKTG 575), Spring 1998.
76. Smith, Michael. Temple University, *Marketing Strategy* (W360), Summer 2001.
77. Solomon, R. Auburn University, *Global Consumer Culture* (CAHS 2000), Spring 2001.
78. Speh, Thomas. Miami University, *Logistics Management* (MKT 431), Spring 2001.
79. Speh, Thomas. Miami University, *Supply Chain Management* (MKT 498), Spring 2001.
80. Stamp, Jeffrey. *Imagination, Entrepreneurship, and Business Problem Solving* (MKT 366), Spring 2001.
81. Stearns, James, Crespy, Charles and Davis, Cindy. Miami University, *Marketing Analysis* (MKT 351), Spring 2001.

82. Tang, Edwin and Lee, Henry. The Asia Pacific Institute of Business, *China Marketing on Internet*, 1997/1998.
83. Taylor, Janice E. Miami University, *Principles of Marketing – Honors* (MKT 291.H), Spring 2001.
84. Taylor, Janice E. Miami University, *Promotion Management* (MKT 441), Spring 2001.
85. Unger, Lynette. Miami University, *Buyer Behavior* (MKT 391), Spring 2001.
86. Vassos, Tom. University of Toronto, *Strategic Internet Marketing*, Fall 1997.
87. Walton, John and Stearns, James. Miami University, *Contemporary Issues in Marketing* (MKT 674), Spring 2001.
88. Westrick, Gregg. Miami University, *Principles of Marketing* (MKT 291), Spring 2001.
89. Widmeyer, George and Rafaeli, Sheizaf. University of Michigan, *Electronic Commerce on the Internet*, Winter 1998.
90. Wright, Newell. James Madison University, *Strategic Marketing on the Internet* (MKTG 498), Summer 1998.
91. Young, Dale. Miami University, *Management Information and Decision Support Systems* (MIS 385), Fall 1998.
92. Young, Ellen S. Miami University, *Advertising and Promotion Management* (MKT 441), Spring 2001.
93. Zimmermann, Paul. Miami University, *Buyer Behavior* (MKT 391), Spring 2001.

**BIBLIOGRAPHY**

Academic Misconduct. Miami University Policy and Information Manual. Section 5.4. http://www.muohio.edu/mupim/ Sections 502 – 505.

Alavi, M., N. Wheeler, and J. Valacich.   Using IT to Reengineer Business Education: An exploratory investigation to collaborative telelearning *MIS Quarterly*, September 1995, pp. 294-312.

Alavi, M. Y. Yoo, and D. Vogel. Using Information Technology to Add Value to Management Education. *Academy of Management Journal* Vol. 40, pp. 1310-33.

Allen, Charlotte. The Virtual University. *Washington Post Magazine* Vol. 10, August 1997. pp. 16-34.

Altman, H.B. Syllabus Shares « What the Teacher Wants. » in M. Weimer & R. A. Neff Teaching College: Collected Readings for the New Instructor (pp. 45-46). Magna Publ.: Madison, WI.

The American Heritage Dictionary – English Language, 4th edition, Bartleby.com   Great   Books   Online.   2000 www.barkleby.com/61/53/S0955300.html

Angelo, Thomas A. and Patrick K. Cross. Classroom Assessment Techniques. Publ. Josey-Bass. San Francisco.

Atwong, Catherine T. and Paul S. Hugstad. Internet Technology and the Future of Marketing Education. *Journal of Marketing Education.* Vol. 19, Nr. 3, 1997. pp. 44-55.

Bailey, E. K, and M. Coltar. Teaching via the Internet. *Communication Education.* Vol. 43 1994. pp. 184-93.

Bannan, Karen J. Multicasting from Satellites Rescues Digital Content from Terrestrial Bottlenecks. Is This the Future of Digital Media Distribution? *Internet World,* July 15, 2001. pp. 50-51.

Beattie, Marc. Streaming and Web Conferencing Integration: Does streaming add to the experience? *E-Learning Magazine,* June 2001. pp. 35 – 38.

Benbunan-Fich,   R.   Leveraging   Management   Education   with Information Technology. *Proceedings of the 36th Annual Meeting of the Eastern Academy of Management.* May 13-16, 1999. Philadelphia, PA.

Benbunan-Fich, R and S. R. Hilz. Educational Applications of CMCS: Solving Case Studies through Synchronous Learning Networks. Journal of Computer-Mediated Communication. Vol. 4. 1999.

Benbunan-Fich, Raquel, Hector R. Lozada, Stephen Pirog, Randi Priluck, and Joseph Wisenblit. Integrating Information Technology into the Marketing Curriculum: A Pragmatic Paradigm. *Journal of Marketing Education,* Vol. 23, Nr. 1, April 2001, pp. 5-15.

Bilmoria, Diana. Emerging Information Technologies and Management Education. *Journal of Management Education.* Vol. 23, 1999. pp. 229-32.

Buchanan, E. A. Assessment measures; Pre-tests for Successful Distance Teaching and Learning: *Online Journal of Distance Learning Administration.* Vol.Nr. 31999.

Canzer, Brahm. Marketing Education on the Internet: A World Wide Web Based Introductory Marketing Course Design for the Virtual Project in Distance Education at Simon Fraser University. *Journal of Marketing Education.* Vol. 19, Fall 1997. pp. 56-65.

Center for Applied Special Technology. Online Use is Growing in Schools. 1996. www.cast.org/udl/index.cfm?:=122

Chariot Software Group. Online Applications for Textbook Publishers: eSyllabus, Software & Services for Testing & Instructional Management. http://www.chariot.com/

Clay, E. and D. VanderBilt. Teaching with a Mission: Using Mission Statements in the Classroom. *Journal on Excellence in College Teaching*, Vol. 8 Nr. 3 1997. pp. 25-39.

Colleges Urged to Use Technology to Promote Lifelong Learning. *Chronicle of Higher Education*, September 24, 1999. A39.

Cooper, Linda. Anatomy of An Online Course. *T H.E Journal*, February, 1999. pp. 49-51.

Curriculum: A Pragmatic Paradigm. *Journal of Marketing Education*, Vol.23, Nr. 1, April 2001, pp. 5-15.

Day, C. W. and N. Nirmalakhandan. Computer Simulation Models in Environmental Engineering Education. Water Science and Technology. Vol. 38 1998. pp. 295-302.

Deveaux, Paul. High-Speed, High-Tech Schools. *E-Learning Magazine,* June 2001. pp. 40 - 43.

Dickson, Gary and A. Segars. Redefining the High-technology classroom. *Journal of Education for Business*. Vol. 73, 1999. pp. 152 – 56.

The Digital Millennium Copyright Act, UCLA Online Institute for Cyberspace Law and Policy, http://www.gseis.ucla.edu/iclp/dmca1.htm

Eastman, Jacqueline K. and Cathy Owens Swift. New Horizons in Distance Education: The Online Learner-Centered Marketing Class. *Journal of Marketing Education*, Vol. 3, Nr. 1, April 2001. pp. 25-34.

Ferrell, O. C. Improving Marketing Education in the 1990s: A Faculty Retrospective and Perspective View. *Marketing Education Review*. Vol. 5, Fall 1995. pp. 69-79.

Florida State University Program for Instructional Excellence. *Construction Of the Syllabus*. www.fsu.edu/~pie/syllabus.html

Garavalia, L. S. Hummel, J.H. Wiley, L.P. and Huitt, W. G. Constructing the Course Syllabus: Faculty and Student Perceptions of Important Syllabus Components. *Journal on Excellence in College Teaching*. Vol. 10 Nr. 1 1999. pp. 5-21.

Gartland, Frank. Implementing Live, Interactive e-learning. *E-Learning Magazine,* June 2001. pp. 18-20.

Gibson, Chere C. Toward Emerging Technologies and Distributed Learning: Challenges and Change. *American Journal of Distance Education*. Vol. 10 1996. pp. 47-49.

Gifford, Jack and Glenn Platt. Building a Comprehensive and Totally Awesome Hardcopy or Electronic Syllabus…plus Integrating and Electronic Scavenger Hunt into your Syllabus. *Miami University Lilly Conference on College Teaching*. November 19-22, 1998. Oxford, Ohio.

Greco, JoAnn. Going the Distance for MBA Candidates. *Journal of Business Strategy.* Vol. 20 Nr. 3 1999. pp. 30-34.

Grunert, Judith. The Course Syllabus: A Learning-Centered Approach. Anker Publishing Company, Inc. Bolton, MA. 1997. ISBN 1-882982-18-5.

Gubernick, Lisa and Ashlea Ebeling. I Got My Degree through E-mail. *Forbes.* Vol 159 1997 Nr. 12. pp. 84-92.

Hankin, J. N.   Alice, the College Teacher, and the Rottweiler in Wonderland: The Prospects and Problems of Distance Learning. *Executive Speeches.* Vol. 14. Nr. 2. pp. 18-21.

Indiana University Purdue University – Indiana Center for Teaching & Learning Resources. Syllabus Construction. www.center.iupui.edu/syllabus_construction.html

Karuppan, Corinne M. and Muthu Karuppan. Empirically Based Guidelines for Developing Teaching Materials on the Web. Business Communications Quarterly. Vol. 62. Nr. 3 1999. pp. 37-45.

Kuechler, M. Using the Web in the Classroom. *Social Science Computer Review.* Vol. 7, 1999. pp. 144-61.

Lawson, Diana S. White and S. Dimitradis. International Business Education and Technology-based Active Learning: Student-reported benefit evaluations. *Journal of Marketing Education.* Vol. 20, 1998. pp. 141-48.

Matejka, K. & Kurke, L. B. Designing a Great Syllabus. *College Teaching* Vol. 42 Nr. 3 1994. pp. 115-117.

McCorkle, Denny E., J. Alexander and James Reardon. Integrating Business Technology and Marketing Education: Enhancing the Diffusion Process through Technology Champions. *Journal of Marketing Education,* Vol. 3, Nr. 1, April 2001. pp. 16-24.

McNeilly, Kevin and Frances Ranney. Combining Writing and the Electronic Media in Sales Management Courses. *Journal of Marketing Education.* Vol. 20, 1998. pp. 226-35.

Miller, Fred and W. G. Mangold. Developing Information Technology Skills in the Marketing Curriculum. *Marketing Education Review.* Vol. 6 Nr. 1, 1996. pp. 29-39.

Moore, M. G. Contemporary Issues in American Distance Learning. Hannon Press, New York 1990.

Netiquette Home Page, The Core Rules of Netiquette, The Netiquette Quiz, A Service of Albion.com. http://www.albion.com/netiquette/

Noble, David F. Digital Diploma Mills – Part II: The Coming Battle Over Online Instruction. *Sociological Perspectives.* Vol. 41. 1998. pp. 815-25.

Palloff, Rena M. and Keith Pratt. Building Learning Communities in Cyberspace. Jossey-Bass Publ: San Francisco, 1999.

Professional Ethics and Responsibilities. Miami University Policy and Information Manual. Section 5.4. http://www.muohio.edu/mupim/5_3.html

Professors Slow to Pick Up Tech Tricks. *MSNBC's Learning Online.* Associated Press, November 15, 1999. www.msnbc.com/news/306031.asp

Ragothaman, Srinvasan, and D. Hoadley. Integrating the Interent and the World Wide Web into the Business Classroom: A Synthesis. *Journal of Education for Business.* Vol. 72, 1997. pp. 213016.

Raths, D. Is Anyone Out There? *Inside Technology Training.* June 1999. pp. 32-34.

Schacter, John. The Impact of Education Technology on Student Achievement. Milken Exchange on Education Technology. www.milkenexchange.org/quick.taf?_function=list&_start=1

Sermersheim, Michael D. Promises to Students. *NACUA Conference.* The University of Akron, June 27, 2000.

Siegel, Carolyn F. Using Computer Networks to Enhance Your Student's Marketing Skills. *Journal of Marketing Education.* Vol. 18, 1996. Nr. 3. pp. 14-24.

The Six Levels of Bloom's Taxonomy of the Cognitive Domain. The National Teaching and Learning Forum. http://www.ntlf.com/html/lib/suppmat/84taxonomy.htm

Smart, Denise, C. Kelley, J. Conant. Marketing Education in the Year 2000: Observed Changes and Challenges Anticipated. *Journal of Marketing Education.* Vol. 21, 1999. pp. 206-16.

Smith, Lois J. Content and Delivery: A Comparison and Contrast of Electronic and Traditional MBA Marketing Planning Courses. *Journal of Marketing Education*, Vol. 3, Nr. 1, April 2001. pp. 35-44.

Stansbery, D. Taking the Plunge. *New Media* February 1993. pp. 30-36.

Statement of Good Teaching Practices. Miami University Policy and Information Manual. Section 5.4. http://www.muohio.edu/mupim/5_4.html

Steinberg, Jacques, and Edward Wyatt. Boola, Boola: E-commerce Comes to the Quad. *New York Times.* February 13, 2000. pp. 1-5.

Sweeney, Jillian C. and Deborah Ingram. A Comparison of Traditional and Web-based Tutorials in Marketing Education: An Exploratory Study. *Journal of Marketing Education*, Vol. 3, Nr. 1, April 2001. pp. 55-62.

Ueltschy, Linda C. An Exploratory Study of Integrating Interactive Technology into the Marketing Curriculum. *Journal of Marketing Education*, Vol. 3, Nr. 1, April 2001. pp. 63-72.

The University of Nebraska – Lincoln Teaching and Learning Center. *Step by Step·Planning a College Course.* http://www.unl.edu/teaching/PlanningCourse.html

The University of Tennesee at Chattanooga Walker Teaching Resource Center. *Syllabus Construction.* http://www.utc.edu/Teaching-Resource-Center/syllabus.html

Woolcock, Michael J.V., *Constructing a Syllabus.* The Harriet W. Sheridan Center for Teaching and Learning, Brown University, undated.

Young, Mark R. Windowed, Wired and Webbed – Now What? *Journal of Marketing Education*, Vol. 3, Nr. 1, April 2001. pp. 45-54.

## APPENDIX B

## THE E-SYLLABUS CHECK SHEET

| CONTENT OR QUESTION TO ANSWER ON E-SYLLABUS | OK | ADD | OMIT |
|---|---|---|---|
| | | | |
| **SECTION ONE: THE HEADER** | | | |
| Course title | | | |
| Course department and number | | | |
| Credit hours (number, fixed, variable) | | | |
| For grade, credit or no credit | | | |
| Semester (Fall, Summer Session I, etc.) | | | |
| Year | | | |
| Course days and time | | | |
| Course location (building and room) | | | |
| Teacher's name and title | | | |
| Program fit (free elective, business core, major, minor, university requirement, divisional requirement, etc.) | | | |
| Prerequisites (courses, class standing, credit hours) | | | |
| Date and time last modified | | | |
| | | | |
| **SECTION TWO: FLASH ANNOUNCEMENTS** | | | |
| Homework reminders | | | |
| Changes in schedule | | | |
| Error corrections | | | |
| Treasure chests | | | |
| | | | |
| **SECTION THREE: TABLE OF CONTENTS MATRIX** | | | |
| Flash announcements | | | |
| Administrative details | | | |
| Justification for level of detail | | | |
| Teaching philosophy | | | |
| Mission, values and vision statements | | | |
| Catalogue description: Current | | | |

| | | | |
|---|---|---|---|
| Catalogue description: Revised | | | |
| Behavioral objectives | | | |
| Communications | | | |
| Pedagogies | | | |
| Faculty and student rights & responsibilities | | | |
| Professional standards of behavior | | | |
| Honesty/Intellectual integrity | | | |
| Attendance | | | |
| Netiquette | | | |
| Grading/Assessment | | | |
| B.A.R.S. | | | |
| Extra credit options | | | |
| Semester calendar of content | | | |
| Table of contents matrix (continued) | | | |
| Daily assignments/learning modules | | | |
| Projects and standards | | | |
| Teams | | | |
| Resources and learning tips | | | |
| Students with disabilities or special circumstances | | | |
| Technical requirements | | | |
| E-suggestion box for | | | |
| Other forms, attachments, acknowledgements, "have read..." forms | | | |
| Caveat statement | | | |
| | | | |
| SECTION FOUR:  ADMINISTRATIVE DETAILS | | | |
| Textbook | | | |
|    Title | | | |
|    Author(s) | | | |
|    Publisher | | | |
|    Edition number and ISBN | | | |
|    Where available: On or off campus | | | |
|      Electronic sources | | | |
|       URLs | | | |
|       Delivery time | | | |
|       Shipping costs | | | |
|       Delivered price | | | |
|    Available only new or also used | | | |

| | | | |
|---|---|---|---|
| Date needed in class | | | |
| Resale information | | | |
| Availability on library reserve | | | |
| Teacher contact information | | | |
| Email address | | | |
| Office phone number and OK hours | | | |
| Home pone number and OK hours | | | |
| FAX number (office and home) | | | |
| Availability of voice mail (office and home) | | | |
| Office building and room number | | | |
| Office hours: | | | |
| Open walk-in hours | | | |
| Sign up office hours (on e-syllabus) | | | |
| Extra office hours before exams & projects due | | | |
| Graduate assistant name and contact information | | | |
| Tutorial materials available and relevant details | | | |
| Other important contact information | | | |
| Student technology labs (people, locations, hours) | | | |
| Course withdrawal policies | | | |
| Teacher: The Professional | | | |
| Teaching interests | | | |
| Degrees, schools, locations | | | |
| Other courses currently/often taught | | | |
| Research interests | | | |
| Recent publications | | | |
| Association memberships | | | |
| Consulting and business experience | | | |
| Committee service (professional, university, division, department, industry, other) | | | |
| Teacher: The Individual | | | |
| Family information and photo album | | | |
| Hobbies | | | |
| What you like to read | | | |
| Music preferences and links | | | |
| Sports interests – doing or watching | | | |
| Travel interests | | | |
| Pets (photo(s)) | | | |
| Religion | | | |

| | | | |
|---|---|---|---|
| Home (photo(s)) | | | |
| Favorite web links, screen savers | | | |
| Places you have lived or traveled | | | |
| You High School | | | |
| Other | | | |
| | | | |
| **SECTION FIVE: JUSTIFICATION FOR DETAIL** | | | |
| Help students understand whys and what's | | | |
| Avoid misunderstandings | | | |
| Faculty documentation | | | |
| Course management tool | | | |
| Two-way communications tool | | | |
| Cognitive course map | | | |
| To create a better, more flexible course | | | |
| To teach and allow the use of information management | | | |
| | | | |
| **SECTION SIX: TEACHING PHILOSOPHY** | | | |
| | | | |
| **SECTION SEVEN: COURSE MISSION, VALUES AND VISION STATEMENTS** | | | |
| Mission statement | | | |
| Value statement | | | |
| Vision statement | | | |
| | | | |
| **SECTION EIGHT: CATALOGUE DESCRIPTION** | | | |
| Current catalogue description | | | |
| Revised catalogue description | | | |
| | | | |
| **SECTION NINE: BEHAVIORAL OBJECTIVES** | | | |
| Cognitive objectives | | | |
| Affective objectives | | | |
| Psychomotor, if any | | | |
| | | | |

| | | | |
|---|---|---|---|
| **SECTION TEN: COMMUNICATIONS** | | | |
| **EMAIL** | | | |
|   **Expected response time** | | | |
|   **Are assignments acceptable as attachments** | | | |
|   **Netiquette email guidelines** | | | |
|   **Student's email on a class email directory ok** | | | |
|   **Established subject header standards required** | | | |
| **TELEPHONE/TELEPHONY/FAX/VOICE MAIL** | | | |
|   **Telephone** | | | |
|       **Number and hours students can call – office** | | | |
|       **Number and hours students can call – home** | | | |
|   **Telephony – software, process and availability** | | | |
|   **FAX** | | | |
|       **Numbers and availability at the office and home** | | | |
|       **Rules for length and use** | | | |
|   **Voice Mail** | | | |
|       **Number and availability at office and home** | | | |
|       **Rules for use** | | | |
| **ELECTRONIC BULLETIN BOARDS** | | | |
|   **Location and access** | | | |
|   **Rules for use and postings** | | | |
|   **Lengths messages may remain on the BB** | | | |
|   **What can and cannot be posted on the BB** | | | |
|   **Netiquette rules and references** | | | |
| **CHAT ROOMS** | | | |
|   **Times chat rooms are open** | | | |
|   **Location and access** | | | |
|   **Rules for use and postings** | | | |
|   **What can and cannot be said in the chat room** | | | |
|   **Netiquette rules and references** | | | |
| **DISCUSSION GROUPS** | | | |
|   **Location and access** | | | |
|   **Rules for use and postings** | | | |

| | | | |
|---|---|---|---|
| Participation levels and frequency | | | |
| Netiquette rules and references | | | |
| Use for making appointments for office hours | | | |
| Twelve hour lead time for office hour appointments | | | |
| | | | |
| **SECTION ELEVEN: PEDAGOGIES** | | | |
| Instructional strategies to be used | | | |
| Why these strategies have been selected | | | |
| Approximate percentage each will be used | | | |
| | | | |
| **SECTION TWELVE: RIGHTS & RESPONSIBILITIES** | | | |
| Faculty rights | | | |
| Faculty responsibilities | | | |
| Student rights | | | |
| Student responsibilities | | | |
| | | | |
| **SECTION THIRTEEN: PROFESSIONAL STANDARDS OF BEHAVIOR, INTELLECTUAL INTEGRITY, ATTENDANCE & NETIQUETTE** | | | |
| Professional standards of behavior | | | |
| Intellectual integrity | | | |
| University divisional and/or dept. II statement | | | |
| University divisional and/or dept. disciplinary standards | | | |
| University, divisional and/or dept. grievance procedures | | | |
| Teacher specific guidelines related to: | | | |
| Homework | | | |
| Project preparation and use | | | |
| Sharing of notes | | | |
| Use of tape recorders in class | | | |
| What constitutes cheating of exams | | | |
| Plagiarism defined; format procedures | | | |
| Availability of past exams | | | |
| Final statement on following regulations | | | |

| | | | |
|---|---|---|---|
| **Attendance** | | | |
| Opening sympathy statement | | | |
| "Cost" of missing class | | | |
| Reasons behind attendance policy | | | |
| How attendance will be taken | | | |
| Maximum number of absences & penalty if exceeded | | | |
| What constitutes excused absences | | | |
| Policy concerning excused absences, documentation   and time limits | | | |
| Policy on notification of non-emergency excused abs. | | | |
| Absences resulting in missed exams or quizzes | | | |
| Penalties for absences | | | |
| **Netiquette** | | | |
| Teacher guidelines | | | |
| Online guidelines | | | |
| | | | |
| **SECTION FOURTEEN: ASSESSMENT, BARS AND EXTRA CREDIT OPTIONS** | | | |
| Assessment | | | |
| Types of assessment tools to be used | | | |
| Relative weights assigned to each assessment tool | | | |
| Dates, times and conditions | | | |
| Points or percentages related to letter grades (table) | | | |
| Do you curve grades? | | | |
| Use of student competition or teacher's standards as grading benchmarks? | | | |
| Do you offer plus/minus grades? | | | |
| Posting of grades, during and at end of semester | | | |
| Use of graduate student in grading? | | | |
| Grading grievance procedure | | | |
| Available examples of past exams | | | |
| Standardized departmental finals | | | |
| Are ID' required at times of exams | | | |
| If student misses an exam – policy | | | |
| Exam review sessions | | | |
| Availability of tutors | | | |

| | | | |
|---|---|---|---|
| Use of peer grades and details | | | |
| Use of individual learning contracts | | | |
| Verbal description of grades A,B,C,D,F | | | |
| Is attendance factored into grades? | | | |
| Self-assessment opportunities or practice exams | | | |
| Policy on the postings of grades | | | |
| Participation grades and B.A.R.S. | | | |
| Behaviorally Anchored Rating Scales | | | |
| Describe BARS and process for creation | | | |
| Describe use, computation, bars and absences | | | |
| Extra Credit Options | | | |
| Describe | | | |
| Potential grade value | | | |
| Due dates | | | |
| How graded | | | |
| | | | |
| SECTION FIFTEEN: CALENDARS AND CONTENT | | | |
| Creation of electronic calendar | | | |
| Presence of hot links | | | |
| Ready designations | | | |
| Class dates | | | |
| Special dates to remember | | | |
| | | | |
| SECTION SIXTEEN: DAILY ASSIGNMENT DETAILS | | | |
| Date | | | |
| Subject matter | | | |
| Relevant behavioral objectives | | | |
| Preparation prior to class | | | |
| Assignments for electronic mediums | | | |
| Resources available for completion of assignment | | | |
| Instructional strategies | | | |
| Material to create or download and bring to class | | | |
| | | | |
| SECTION SEVENTEEN: PROJECTS, STANDARDS, GUIDELINES AND | | | |

| | | | |
|---|---|---|---|
| **SUGGESTED TIMELINES** | | | |
| For each project or assignment: | | | |
| Behavioral objectives | | | |
| Individual or team effort | | | |
| If group, explain or relevant processes | | | |
| Time line: start, stages, due date and time | | | |
| How will project be graded; standards | | | |
| Format and technical requirements | | | |
| Available guidelines (written, oral, other) | | | |
| Availability of past project; where | | | |
| Penalties of submitted late; define late | | | |
| Suggested do's and don'ts | | | |
| | | | |
| **SECTION EIGHTEEN: USE OF TEAMS** | | | |
| How will the teams be formed? | | | |
| If cannot find a team, options? | | | |
| Team size | | | |
| Behavioral objectives | | | |
| Availability of electronic media | | | |
| Progress reports and meetings with teacher | | | |
| Required work logs | | | |
| TEAMS (continued) | | | |
| Format of team output? | | | |
| How will team projects be graded? | | | |
| Can team members be fired? Process? | | | |
| Options open to fired members? | | | |
| Will peer reviews be used and if so, how? | | | |
| Can teams be formed beyond a single class section? | | | |
| | | | |
| **SECTION NINETEEN: RESOURCES AND LEARNING TIPS** | | | |
| Electronic resources | | | |
| Print resources | | | |
| Human resources | | | |
| Learning tips | | | |
| | | | |
| **SECTION TWENTY: STUDENTS WITH DISABILITIES AND SPECIAL CIRCUMSTANCES** | | | |

| | | | |
|---|---|---|---|
| How and when you are to be notified | | | |
| Documentation required | | | |
| Approved absences due to special circumstances: | | | |
|     Family emergency – process required | | | |
|     Personal illness – process required | | | |
|     Religious holidays – process required | | | |
|     University sanctioned functions - process | | | |
| | | | |
| SECTION TWENTY ONE: TECHNICAL CLASS REQUIREMENTS | | | |
| | | | |
| SECTION TWENTY TWO: THE E-SUGGESTION BOX | | | |
| | | | |
| SECTION TWENTY THREE: FORMS, STUDENT INFORMATION SHEETS, ACKNOWLEDGEMENTS, HAVE READ FORMS | | | |
| Forms to facilitate classroom assignments | | | |
| Have read... form | | | |
| Student Information sheet | | | |
|     Full name | | | |
|     Name they wish to be called in class | | | |
|     Major and minor | | | |
|     Credit hours completed to date | | | |
|     University address | | | |
|     Home address | | | |
|     Current telephone number and email address | | | |
|     Photo attachment | | | |
|     Job experiences to date (company and position) | | | |
|     Immediate family business experience | | | |
|     Emergency medical condition | | | |
|     Interviewing intensions (industry, companies) | | | |
|     "Two things that make me unique" | | | |
|     Birthday – date and year | | | |
| | | | |

## APPENDIX  C

## EXAMPLE E-SYLLABUS

MARKETING STRATEGY 491
DEPARTMENT OF MARKETING
RICHARD T. FARMER SCHOOL OF BUSINESS
ADMINISTRATION
MIAMI UNIVERSITY (OHIO)
FALL 2002

Teacher: Professor John (Jack) B. Gifford
Days & Times: Tuesdays/Thursdays 3:30 - 4:45 pm
Place: Upham 209
Credit Hours: (3) <u>Heavy</u> Fixed [May NOT be audited or taken for credit /no credit]
Program Credit: LE Capstone, SBA Capstone, Marketing Capstone
Prerequisites: Marketing 291 and Senior Standing (96 hours completed)

FLASH ANNOUNCEMENTS

The first three weeks set the stage for the rest of the semester. It is <u>extremely important</u> to you to understand and be able to apply the concepts, processes and quantitative skills presented during the first six class periods!  Also lots of class preparation will be essential!

**Table of Contents Navigational Matrix**

| Main Schedule of Activities Shortcut | | |
|---|---|---|
| Flash Announcements | Administrative Details | Justification for Level of Detail |
| Teaching Philosophy | Catalogue Description and Revision | Behavioral Objectives |
| Communications | Instructional Strategies | Faculty and Student Rights and Responsibilities |
| Professional Standards of Behavior | Intellectual Integrity | Attendance |
| Do's and Don'ts | Assessment and Grading | B.A.R.S |
| Dropping a Course | Teams | Resources and Learning Tips |
| Students with Disabilities or Special Needs | E-Suggestion Box Form | Have-Read Form |
| Information Form | | |

## ADMINISTRATIVE DETAILS

**Textbook**

Cases in Strategic Marketing, David Rosenthal and Lew G. Brown
Prentice Hall, 2000; Edition: First; ISBN: 0-13-086359-9
Available new or used:
DuBois and University Bookstores
Online: www.amazon.com and www.barnesandnoble.com
Needed by August 26th

**Teacher Contact Information**

John (Jack) B. Gifford, Professor of Marketing
Email: GIFFORJB@MUOHIO.EDU
Telephone (Office): 513-529-1207 (8-5 M-R; V-Mail Available)
FAX (Office): 513-529-1290 (any time 8-5 M-F)
Office: Upham 206A
Telephone (Home): 513-523-2227 (Sun-Th. 7–9:30 pm)
Home Web Page www.sba.muohio.edu/GIFFORJB/index.htm
Syllabus links
Professional links
Information Links
Professional Resume Information
Gifford After Hours Photos and Activities
Office Hours: Upham 206A
M,W 7:45-11:45 am
T, R 9:30-10:30 am
or by appointment
No Office Hours on  Fridays
Mailbox: Upham 200 (first row, left side, near windows)
US Mail (Office)
Professor John B. Gifford
Department of Marketing  Upham 200
Richard T. Farmer School of Business Administration
Miami University
Oxford, Ohio 4556
US Mail (Home)
Professor John B. Gifford
6511 Morning Sun Road
Oxford, Ohio 45056
Graduate Assistant: T.B.A.
Example Exam Case: See file in Upham 200 after September 10th.
Do not copy or remove.
Secretary: Ruth Lucas, Upham 200 Front Desk

## Course withdrawal policies

- You can withdraw with a grade of "W" until December 6 [th] at 5:00 pm unless regulations are changed;
- You will receive a "WP" if your grade point to date is 72.5% or better and you have not missed six classes or more;
- You will receive a "WF" or "F" if your grade point to date is under 70% or you have missed six or more classes for any reason.

*NOTE: A revised university wide policy has been passed by the University Senate in the Spring of 2001, was then withdrawn, and is now again under discussion. Exact status is unknown. The above dates and policies are subject to change depending upon the timing and nature of the outcome of this university wide regulation*

### JUSTIFICATION FOR DETAILED SYLLABUS

There are seven reasons I have created a longer than usual e-syllabus:

- If you are taking Marketing 491 as an elective, this e-syllabus will give you enough information to decide if you wish to stay or find an alternative course. You should have enough information to permit an "eyes open" enrollment in the course. It will require a lot of homework (8+) every week to learn and succeed.
- By spelling out procedures on grading, attendance, participation grades, teams, etc. I have tried to avoid misunderstandings later in the course. For example, if you miss six classes or more for any reason, you will receive a failing grade.
- All faculty have been asked to document their teaching efforts in a "Teaching Portfolio". This policy has been mandated by the university, the School of Business Administration, and the Department of Marketing. A complete syllabus is the heart and soul of any teaching portfolio.
- The creation of a well-designed syllabus acts as an effective course management tool. It also acts as a cognitive map of the course.
- This e-syllabus acts as a medium of two- way communication. It allows you to access resources, coordinate with colleagues electronically, have access to flash announcements, and download URL sites, word and excel files, and other electronic resources that will support this class.
- An e-syllabus allows me to make changes as we go along that respond to your demonstrated needs. For example, If you are struggling with interpreting strategic decision-making or logistics

problems in foreign countries, I can change cases later in the semester that give you more international logistics learning opportunities.

## TEACHING PHILOSOPHY

I believe that higher education, including this course, has as a primary objective the development of life long active learners who make the world a better place to live one person at a time. The emphasis is on the skills of problem solving and decision-making in environments of uncertainty and incomplete information, with a significant secondary emphasis on the acquisition of new knowledge. The course will also demand that you apply your skills and knowledge from all the courses you have taken, plus that you learn from your colleagues and me. Learning involves hard work, good listening, written and oral communication skills, a willingness to change and challenge your own predispositions, and always to think with your mind, feelings and heart. Ethics are involved in almost every decision you make in your life…and in your responses to the case studies and class negotiations in this course.

Knowledge and skills without application, comprehension, analysis, synthesis and evaluation are of marginal benefit to you, your employer, your own business, or society. In this course, a senior capstone, higher-level thinking (synthesis, application, evaluation) is essential.

Lastly, college is about maturing, learning, give and take, and having fun in the process. Don't stress out! Working hard and having fun are compatible activities. <u>This course will require at least 10-12 total hours of your time a week</u>. It is your last opportunity in college to put everything together in one class. Your personal and professional growth during the semester for some of you may well make the difference between becoming a shooting star or so-so decision maker in business…and life.

I teach because it is a tremendous high to see the progress most of you make in solving problems and decision making between the first and last weeks of the semester. You learn to see the forest and individual trees, flowers and weeds. I also thoroughly enjoy interacting with such bright and unique individuals on a daily basis. Oh yes, and I also get paid!

## MISSIONS, VALUES, AND VISION STATEMENTS

**Mission Statement**

The mission of Marketing 491 is to significantly improve your higher order learning skills involved in ethical decision-making and problem solving in a variety of domestic and international business environments under conditions of risk, uncertainty and incomplete information.

Also see Mission Statements of

Miami University:

http://www.miami.muohio.edu/Documents_and_Policies/missionstatement/index.cfm

the SBA:

http://www.sba.muohio.edu/HOME/missionstatement.htm

and Department of Marketing:

http://www.netgain.muohio.edu/MARKETING/ACADEMICS/MISSION.HTML

**Miami University Value Statement 2002**

Miami is a scholarly community whose members believe that a liberal education is grounded in qualities of character as well as of intellect. We respect the dignity of other persons, the rights and property of others, and the right of others to hold and express disparate beliefs. We believe in honesty, integrity and the importance of moral conduct. We defend the freedom of inquiry that is the heart of learning and combine that freedom with the exercise of judgment and the acceptance of personal responsibility.

Course Value Statement: In Marketing 491, we will value careful and detailed conversion of data into information, knowledge and wisdom designed to objectively identify SWOT$^s$, the Problem Statement, Alternatives, Criteria, followed by insightful Analysis, Recommendations and Implementation. All the above must be accomplished in a multidisciplinary environment, communicated effectively and efficiently, and moderated by sound and consistent ethical foundations.

**Course Vision Statement**

In 85% of Marketing 491 you will act as the principal decision-makers of actual business decisions reported in case studies. You will individually and collectively take responsibility for making the "best" decision and implementation recommendations possible based upon a thorough and insightful analysis, synthesis and evaluation of available data and information. In most cases, either somewhat dated or unfamiliar industries will be the topics of discussion to emphasize process.

## COURSE DESCRIPTIONS

### University Bulletin
Capstone core course deals in depth with domestic and international problems in all areas of marketing. Considers impact of technology and ethics on these problems. Focuses on development and application of analysis framework.

### Improved and Revised Bulletin Course Description
Capstone course deals in depth and breadth with domestic and international problems in all areas of business, with primary emphasis in marketing. We will value careful and detailed conversion of data into information and then knowledge and wisdom designed to objectively identify all dimensions of the *Decision Process*. All the above will be accomplished in a multidisciplinary environment, communicated effectively and efficiently, and moderated by sound and consistent ethical foundations.

## BEHAVIORAL OBJECTIVES

1.  To develop your problem solving and analytical decision making skills within a domestic or international business context;
2.  To develop communication skills through presentations and defense of ideas and analysis before a critical audience in both written and oral forms;
3.  To expand and increase your knowledge of marketing and to assist you in diagnosing, synthesizing and applying your existing knowledge to complex national and international marketing situations;
4.  To be able to understand and discuss intelligently some current issues and conditions in marketing and business in general;
5.  To know and apply the components involved in Strategic Marketing Management Model at a preliminary level;
6.  To assist you in developing the following diagnostic skills:
    a.  Environmental (SWOT) Scans
    b.  Problem Definition
    c.  Recognition of Alternatives

      d. Establishment of Criteria/Objectives/Benchmarks
      e. The Analysis of Alternatives against Criteria
      f. Conclusions and Recommendations
      g. Implementation Strategies

7. To help you develop an understanding of, and appreciation for, the marketing profession and the role that mktg. plays in business & society;

8. To stimulate and refine your ability to see the implications of dynamic environments as creative business opportunities;

9. To stimulate a Socratic and participative approach to learning;

10. To stimulate a habit and hunger for life-long learning;

11. To encourage you to extend your learning horizons beyond the classroom and into the business community and professional literature. I would strongly suggest you start reading the *Wall Street Journal, Fortune, Business Week*, and *Forbes* plus one function specific publication (*Stores, Banking, Fulfillment & Operations*, Advertising Age, Women's Wear Daily, etc.).

12. To emphasize teamwork and sharing as a means to developing a supportive learning environment. You are not in competition with your classmates, but with yourself and with the standards for learning set by me.

13. To help prepare you for the transition from the real world of the university to the real world of professional full-time employment.

14. To stimulate an appreciation for and develop of an individual model applied to moral dimensions of business decision making;

15. To have fun learning together. School should be considered a challenge and an opportunity to be appreciated and enjoyed, not tolerated. Less that one out of five hundred of the worlds' population has the opportunity to complete a college education. You are one of these fortunate individuals!

## COMMUNICATIONS

**Email:** GIFFORJB@MUOHIO.EDU

You are welcome to email me any time, night or day. I normally do not check my email after 5:00 pm and only sometimes on weekends. From Monday to Friday I will usually check at least four times a day; once early in the morning, mid morning, once after lunch, and a fourth time around 4:45 pm. I will try to respond within 24 hours during the work week. Please always use in the subject line FIRSTNAME_LASTNAME_MKT491. Attachments will normally not be opened due to the danger of accidental .exe virus contamination. Please keep your messages concise and specific. I often receive 40+ emails a day. I will use your return address to respond. Use appropriate Netiquette. http://www.albion.com/netiquette/index.html

**Phone/Voice Mail** : (Home) 513-523-2227; (Office) 513-529-1207
You are welcome to call the office anytime Monday through Friday between 8:00 am and 4:30 pm. If I am not there or the line is busy, please leave a voice mail and I will get back to you. Students in the office always have priority over incoming calls unless I believe the call may be from a member of my family. Be sure to leave you telephone number…and say it twice, slowly and clearly. I am usually available at home Monday through Thursday in the evenings and on weekends if needed. I do not have a cell phone.

**FAX**: 513-529-1290
The above FAX number is used by the entire department and is located in Upham 200. Normally our student assistants will place incoming FAX messages in individual mailboxes upon receipt. Be sure to place my name and the course number somewhere at the top of the first page so that the staff can identify the intended recipient. Don't send anything that is personal or confidential in nature. Also, do not send homework via this medium as delivery is less then 100% reliable.

**Electronic Bulletin Board**:
If you are looking for help from a colleague on any non-exam case study, financial numbers, looking for an exam partner, or trying to sell or buy a "whatever," you are welcome to post a note on the Bulletin Board in Blackboard. This will only work if everyone visits the BB on a fairly regular basis. Please date and add you're your name to all posting. I will generally remove all messages that are more then 10 days old. Anything reasonable, ethical and in good taste is acceptable. I do reserve the right to remove anything, anytime, for any reason…but probably won't. Unfortunately, this system has not worked well in the past as the majority of you do not visit the blackboard site on a regular basis.

**Discussion Groups and Chat Rooms**:
At this time I do not plan on using Blackboard discussion questions or chat rooms except maybe for one or two assignments. Some discussion questions and case hints will often appear in the Daily Assignment Descriptions (DAD) or in FLASH ANNOUNCEMENTS

in this e-syllabus and/or as an announcement on Blackboard.. Spreadsheets using Excel will appear in DAD as electronic links to the "G" public drive. You can reach this drive through MUNET by entering "GDRIVE.SBA.MUOHIO.EDU." ALWAYS download the assignment before starting your work. This is very important as you can mess up dozens of your colleagues if you make changes on the master copy. If you have suggestions how we might collectively use these electronic functions better, please send me an E-Suggestion or talk to me before or after class or during office hours. Thanks.

## INSTRUCTIONAL STRATEGIES

### Case Method

The primary instructional strategy to be used in Marketing 491 is the case analysis. This will occupy 85% of our time. There will only be three lectures (10%) during the entire semester (day two plus marketing strategy lectures). As part of the case study method, small groups will often be used at the beginning of the class, followed by presentations by each group using overheads, chalkboards, computers and/or oral presentations.

Near the end of the semester we will spend approximately 4 class periods negotiating and writing a contract for a business-to-business transaction off the coast of Texas. This will involve six or seven teams, each including three buyers and three sellers. More details will be provided in the Daily Assignment Descriptions for weeks 13 and 14. Your contract and participation in this exercise will be 4% of your semester grade.

Our case studies will cover a very broad range of marketing topics such as segmentation, international channels of distribution, strategic planning, organization to organization marketing, new product introductions, pricing, promotion, customer behavior, retailing, wholesaling, logistics, service marketing, acquisitions, aqua-business, production & operations management, non-profit marketing, leisure industry, e-commerce, high technology marketing and marketing research. Some of these cases will take place in international settings. While dealing with these topics, your entire range of marketing, economic, finance, accounting, management, business law, MIS and DSC skills and knowledge will be required. While our primary emphasis will be marketing management and strategy, this can never be isolated from all the other functional areas in business. In fact, as both a Liberal Education and School of Business Administration Capstone, the emphasis MUST involve both horizontal and vertical knowledge and skill integration.

Fifteen to 18 short homework assignments will be given throughout the semester. These will be collected and graded. You are also expected to carefully prepare each case study before class, and to bring a complete set of detailed hand written case discussion notes. This will take a minimum of four hours per class period. These case notes may be collected on a random basis! We also may have a short mini-quiz (part of participation grade) at any time to help me understand how well you are preparing for the cases.

Two case exams and a final are listed in the syllabus and are to be completed outside the classroom (except the final). They must be prepared completely on your own without assistance from any human source besides your two partners. You must select different partners for each of the first two exam cases. At the end of each of the exam cases must appear the following signed statement, *"We have worked entirely alone on this case without written or oral assistance from anyone "* followed by your signatures. These cases must be typed, a maximum of nine main body pages and maximum of 9 pages in appendices, 12 point Arial typeset, plus a cover page (Names, Section, & Soc. Sec. Nrs.) and Table of Contents with page numbers. A handout will be provided with additional guidelines.

The final exam will be on Monday, December 9th from 7:35 to 10:45 pm. It will be open book and open notes; however, the specific case will not be announced until the time of the exam. You can again work in threes for this exam and may select any of your prior partners or someone new. We will work in the computer lab (Laws 207) as the "classroom" for the final. Each team of three will have two or three computers available to them unless you bring your own portable. The number will be determined by the number of computers up-and-running and the size of the class.

The case method has been selected as the primary instructional strategy as it permits you to act in a management decision-making role. All the cases are real, although the names or data may have been disguised to protect the confidentiality of the company. In some cases, we will create our own live case, or expand upon a written case, using supplemental information. In our discussions of strategic planning, we will use a real company as our subject. This method involves a heavy responsibility on your part for proactive learning, careful preparation of notes, and contributions to your group and the class as a whole.

## RIGHTS AND RESPONSIBILITIES

**My Roles and Responsibilities as a Teacher**

It is my responsibility to create a total learning environment where you are actively encouraged to question, acquire specific cognitive information, evaluate alternative careers and lifestyles, values, attitudes and beliefs, and to improve your communication skills. I will attempt to be a positive role model and maintain high personal ethical standards. As a teacher, I have been entrusted by your parents or guardians with helping to prepare you to live full and valued lives. I accept this responsibility. I will in class ten minutes before and after the class each day and will provide each student with a comprehensive electronic course syllabus (THIS IS IT) that contains relevant student guidelines. I will always be fully prepared to guide the discussions of all cases and will set the stage and parameters for all special activities where appropriate. My primary teaching pedagogy is to design a learning environment where active learning from your colleagues is a primary component. I will act as guide and consultant, but will not usually attempt force-feeding. Again, you are responsible for your own learning.

I will carefully grade all classroom exercises, cases and exams, and return all materials in a timely manner (within 7 working days). I will make myself available a minimum of 10 hours per week outside class to assist you in resolving problems you may be having with course materials or career decisions. I will share with you some of my insights from teaching, consulting and working in marketing for the past 35 years when relevant to course learning objectives. I will regularly assess your performance toward the stated course objectives, and will keep you informed of how you are doing.

It is my responsibility to remain current in my subject fields and the teaching profession. It is my responsibility as a scholar teacher to synthesize and assimilate existing knowledge, generate new knowledge, regularly interact with practitioners and other academics, and to take personal responsibility for the improvement of my teaching skills and when asked, the teaching of my colleagues. I will follow all ethical rules of Miami University and the Student Handbook, with particular attention to "Good Teaching Practices."

**Your Roles, Rights and Responsibilities as a Student**

It is the responsibility of each of you to attend all regularly scheduled classes. You should bring extensive notes to class each day that reflect your best thinking about the topic assigned for the day. This "class" should be treated as a business meeting where you are consultants to a variety of executives. In business, you would never show up late or unprepared for such an important meeting! Your academic colleagues and I expect the same. You should actively and regularly share your insights, questions and ideas with your teacher and colleagues. All papers, cases, case notes and projects should be turned in on time and in the format assigned. You should take on the responsibility of helping your peers to learn when necessary through the sharing of your knowledge and opinions. You will not knowingly cheat in any way. Placing your name on an assignment that is not your work is dishonest.

If you have suggestions for a better way to stimulate learning in class or are unhappy with any activities of your teacher or fellow students, it is your responsibility to let the teacher know. You are paying a large amount of money to attend each class at Miami University, and have a right to expect your teachers to fulfill their responsibilities identified above. Learning is an active, not passive process. This year may be your last chance to make mistakes without the very real threat of career damage. Make your mistakes now, and then learn from them. A more formal class review will be conducted one week after the first exam to gather feedback on "I like..." and "I wish...".

## INTELLECTUAL INTEGRITY, ATTENDANCE, PROFESSIONAL BEHAVIOR

### Intellectual Integrity

I assume that everyone is honest unless proven otherwise. You are encouraged to work in small groups on all non-exam cases unless specifically told otherwise. Work on the exam cases must be done on your own with your partners. You may not ask for help from any third party or refer to any notes that others might have prepared for cases in the past. If you wish to combine any non-case written work in this class with something required by another faculty member, I will normally have no objection, provided that you submit, in writing, a statement of this intent to both faculty members prior to submitting your work to either individual. A violation of any of the above will be considered dishonest.

In the negotiation simulation, you are not to show anyone, including your team members, your script. Doing so is considered dishonest. You may share verbally as much of the information as you feel appropriate to achieve your personal and team objectives.

# The Syllabus / E-Syllabus for the 21st Century 101

Using notes from past students is considered dishonest. Signing someone else's name on the attendance sheet is an act of dishonesty.

One copy of a past exam will be placed on reserve in Upham 200 starting on the third week of class. You may read and take notes, but do not copy or remove this exam case from Upham 200. Dishonesty on any of the exam cases will result in an "F" in the course and potentially a dishonestly notation on your transcript. It may result in dismissal from Miami University. Dishonesty on a daily assignment will result in a 0% on that assignment. In cases of dishonesty, the regulations of the Department of Marketing, the Division and the University will be followed to the letter. Please don't risk your own self-respect and graduation by cheating. You cannot cheat your colleagues or me; you can only cheat yourself. Unfortunately, I am obligated by university regulations to take action if dishonesty is discovered. See http://www.muohio.edu/univpubs/handbook/acadregsp V.html for university intellectual integrity policy, Sections 500 to 507apply.

PS: This course is not offered in the summer, nor can it be transferred from another institution because it is a LE & SBA capstone. If you cheat on an exam and are a Marketing major, you must retake the course at Miami University.

**Attendance**

A number of learning opportunities will be made available which cannot be adequately obtained from simply reading the textbooks, cases or handouts. If you are an out-of-state student, you are paying approximately $68.00 per class period (assumes 16 hours of classes per semester). We also need your active participation and expertise to be shared with your fellow students and myself. For these reasons, class attendance is very important, and will be taken starting August 22nd. Participation grades are given daily; therefore, if you are not there, your participation grade for that day will be 50%. If you decline an "invitation" to present, you will receive 50%. If you are not prepared, it is best to let me know before the class starts. In this case, your name will not be drawn from the jar, but you will receive a 65% for the day's participation.

Class will start promptly at 3:45 pm. It would be unprofessional to be late! If you are more then 10 minutes late, you are absent. If you must miss a class, your 50% participation grade can be replaced by a five-page typed case analysis or similar learning opportunity appropriate to the subject missed. This will be due by 5:00 pm within five calendar days of the class missed . This paper is intended to be a substitute learning opportunity and not a penalty.

Every class period has been designed as a piece of a larger mosaic/puzzle and I do not want you leaving this class without at least being exposed to all the pieces. It is your responsibility to submit the paper or come up with a worthwhile substitute learning opportunity if a case was not covered on that date. No reminders will be given. You are adults. If you miss six class periods or more for any reason, even with makeup papers, you will receive an "F" for the course.

Attendance is taken by your signing the attendance sheet placed next to the door every class period. If you do not sign in, you are presumed not to be in class.

I am not in the business of judging if your absence is "excused" or "unexcused", whatever this means. You are there or are not there. If you are sick, have a personal emergency, interviews or varsity sports, there is a method specified above for replacing the 50% grade with an appropriate letter grade. If there is a strong chance that you will be absent more then five times during the semester, you should not take this section of the course. As illness or personal emergencies are unpredictable, it would be very unwise to "cut" class a number of times early in the semester. As a marketing major, you cannot graduate without MKT 491, and it is not offered in the summer. It can also not be transferred from another university, as it is a Liberal Education and SBA Capstone.

**Professional Behavior**

Think of our classroom as a corporate planning meeting. The other students are your professional colleagues from your corporation. I am the individual who has called the meeting and who is responsible for seeing that good decisions are made for the corporation and executives involved. Address others by name (everyone will have a name card every day). Listen to what they have to say. Agree or disagree and explain why. Alternate taking the various roles common in groups such as leader, facilitator, peacemaker, change agent, or follower. Share your ideas with your team and your colleagues. When working on an exam case, all three individuals will need to give 150% to be successful. You are also partially responsible for the success of others in the class. Avoid profanity and sexist or racially negative statements and stereotypes. Your class participation grades result not only from your contributions to the class as a whole, but your ability to move your group and class discussion forward in its' tasks. No inactive sponges allowed!

When using electronic communication medium, proofread your message before it is sent. In industry, you will be judged by how you communicate electronically. Use good Netiquette.

## ASSESSMENT AND B.A.R.S.

**Grading**

Grades are, unfortunately, a necessity of our present academic system. They are designed to measure your level of attainment rather than the degree of change in your cognitive and affective knowledge and skills achieved during a specific class. You are not in competition with your fellow students, as grades are not given on a competitive basis. You will be graded against absolute learning objectives established by myself for this course. This means there is no curve or predetermined number of students who receive A, B, C, D or F grades. Grades measure output, not input; however, these are normally highly related concepts. If everyone in class does an outstanding job, everyone will receive a high grade.

I believe the current system has made both students and teachers too grade oriented, and would encourage you to work diligently toward increased knowledge and understanding; appropriate grades will normally follow. I consider the average Miami University senior to be of very high caliber. A student wishing to receive an "A/A-" must do outstanding work throughout the semester, always going one step or more beyond that asked of her or him. An "F" student is one who rarely makes worthwhile contributions in class, does very poorly on the case exams, displays a lack of interest, curiosity, desire and ability to master the materials presented, is dishonest, or misses class six times or more for any reason.

During the Spring, 2002 semester, the course grade average in my three sections was 2.98. It is usually around a 2.85.

Grades will be given based upon the following distribution of points. Grading on each case will become progressively more challenging as you gain experience. Therefore, a case, which might receive a "C+" during the fifth week, might well receive a "C-" in the tenth week. I expect you to grow and learn from each case.

Grades will be computed as follows:

| | |
|---|---|
| Case Exam #1 | 24% |
| Case Exam #2 | 30% |
| Final Case Exam | 17% |
| Participation | 21% |
| Negotiation | 4% |
| Marketing Metric I +II | 4% |

---------------------------------------------------------------

| | |
|---|---|
| TOTAL | 100% |

| | |
|---|---|
| A+ | 97.01 or more |
| A | 92.31-97.00 |
| A- | 92.30-89-50 |
| B+ | 87.5-89.49 |
| B | 82.50-87.49 |
| B- | 80.00-82.49 |
| C+ | 77.50-79.99 |
| C | 72.50-77.49 |
| C- | 70.00-72.49 |
| D+ | 67.50-69.99 |
| D | 64.50-67.49 |
| D- | 62.50-64.49 |

| | |
|---|---|
| F | Under 62.49%, dishonesty, or missing more than 5 classes |
| WP | See earlier comments |
| WF | See earlier comments |

# The Syllabus / E-Syllabus for the 21st Century 105

Two case exams appear on the *Calendar and Content Matrix* that follows. They are to be completed in teams of three, with different partners required for each of the cases. This will give you an opportunity to experience four different individual's thinking processes and communication styles. The final exam will be handed out at the time of the final. You may select any of your prior partners or new ones for the final. The two case exams must be completed according to the guidelines provided on the second day of class in the Case Methods Packet and this e-syllabus. On the day they are due, it will be the case under discussion for that class period. You will be graded on both the quality of your thought processes, the quality of your presentation, the correctness of your analysis, and your written communication skills. Always carefully proofread your paper. Professional tables, charts, and graphics are expected. Sloppy and imprecise wording can be disastrous in business. For example, a criteria that "the company achieve a 9% ROI" lacks precision as ROI can be computed in 8 ways and no time is stated for achieving the ROI. Is this ROI overall, this division, or this new product introduction? Be sure to use the lexicon of your profession that you have acquired over the past several years.

The final exam will be completed in the computer labs in LAWS 207. It will be open book, notes, etc. You may bring a supplemental laptop if you wish. You may not ask for outside help via email or other communications media during the final. Your final exam will need to end up on a single disk and a single file to be graded. You will participate near the end of the semester in a negotiation simulation. You will be graded on achieving a win-win contract that is both complete and concise. No loopholes! The grading criteria will be discussed more fully the day that the individual player scripts are distributed. It is very important NOT to miss any of these class periods, as your character will have information that no one else possesses.

Exam cases are not accepted late, defined as 5:00 pm of the day they are first discussed. Each member of the your team should have a copy for use during the class(es) for reference during discussion, I will grade all exam cases. My graduate assistant will grade some of the short, daily papers, such as the financial computations in the second week and some spreadsheets. Participation grades will be recorded for every class period starting the second week of class. The B.A.R.S. scale (see below) will be used as the basis for judging your level of performance in class, plus mini-quizzes, and the short assignments made throughout the class.

## Behaviorally Anchored Rating Scales (B.A.R.S.)

B.A.R.S. represent a method by which objectivity and consistency can be improved, but not guaranteed, in the recording of participation grades. You will also understand what you have to do to receive good participation grades and the difference between the quantity and quality of "verbiage" displayed in class.

The process of creating a B.A.R.S. scale will take about 15 minutes of class time. In class, your group will be asked to write down observable behaviors that occur during a discussion that represents excellent, very good, average, poor or very poor contributions to the achievement of defined class behavioral objectives. For example, if a student repeats a point just made, this contributes nothing to the discussion, indicates that the student was not an active listener, and would be judged as a "very poor" contribution. On the other hand, a student who shares a unique and overlooked insight, process or observation that moves the discussion forward for every one would be judged excellent. The repeating of a case fact, converted into useful information might be a good contribution. The fact alone without interpretation and implications might be rated somewhere between average and poor. I will add my own B.A.R.S. to the list and then distribute a final B.A.R.S. Evaluation Form to you by August 27th[th]. This will represent the observable behavioral standards I will attempt to use during the semester. Although my memory is imperfect as to exactly who said what, I have confidence that the cumulative 25+ participation grades will "be in the ballpark". I will give you feedback on your participation grades to date three times during the semester.

## DROPPING A COURSE

### Student Handbook 203e

*"When a full semester course is dropped within three calendar weeks from the date when chasses begin, no grade will appear on the student's record When a full semester course is dropped after the third week of classes and before the end of the sixth week of classes, a grade of "W" will be recorded on the student's academic record. A grade of "WP" will be recorded for those students who drop a course after six weeks if they are passing the course with a grade of "C" or better. If the instructor drops a student after the sixth week by class roster or memo, a "WF" is recorded on the student's record."*

## SUGGESTED DO'S AND DON'TS

Find a partner for the first exam as soon as possible. Start working on the first exam case by the end of the second week.

Work both alone and with one or more partners on non-exam cases. Two or more hard working minds will get you past some of the dead ends and quantitative frustrations you will otherwise encounter.

If an exam partner is not working out, fire the person and find someone else ASAP. These cases are too complex to be completed by 2 ¼ people; don't tolerate free rides!

Plan on this course taking up ¼ of your academic time this semester. An average week will be about 10-12 hours, but some weeks will require more time. The last two weeks are designed to be much easier.

Work particularly hard on the number crunching during the second week. A solid understanding of all the handouts and the problems will save you a lot of headaches throughout the semester. Also Croft and Johnson & Quinn provide valuable lessons in quantitative analysis. You will see some of this material in every single case we do during the next 15 weeks.

When you feel like giving up on a case, give a colleague a call and hopefully they can point you in the right direction. This is definitely a course where you only get in proportion to what you invest in time and energy. Next year you will be solving problems and conducting this type of analysis in the business world or graduate school.

## TEAMS

We will be using three types of teams during this class. The first type of team will be build around the table you select in class. You are welcome to change tables each class period or to stay with the same people each time. As the number of people working on a specific problem will change, depending upon the opening activities for that class period, it will be impossible to have exactly the same people and number each day. Be sure to select a table that is diverse in terms of skill sets, personalities, and gender balance.

The second types of team we will have are teams of three for preparing the three exams. These teams should always be composed of at least one person who is strong in interpreting data and information manipulation and a second person who writes extremely well and can maintain a focused and broad perspective at the same time. Pick your partners early and start on the exam case at least 2-3 weeks before it is due. If your partners are unwilling to do 150% of her or his share in the first week, change partners.

The third type of teams will be the negotiation teams during the last two weeks of class after spring break. I will carefully build these teams to hopefully achieve a balance of strengths and weaknesses both within and between the buyers and sellers. Participate fully. Decide on the roles you will play in terms of facilitating a successful meeting of the minds. Do not miss any of these three classes. Make reasonable win-win-win concessions. In fact, one player must not achieve any of their objectives in order to successfully complete their role!

By this time all of you have participated in a number of group projects. Some of you have also taken negotiation, leadership, or studied group dynamics in your management classes. Put this knowledge to work. In this exercise, it takes all the members signatures to have a valid contract. You cannot fire a member of your team if they are not contributing, or actually getting in the way. It is up to you, collectively, to keep everyone involved and headed in the right direction.

## STUDENTS WITH DISABILITIES OR SPECIAL NEEDS

If you have a physical or learning disability that has been documented and will require some accommodation during this class, you must let me know in the first two weeks. We will meet together privately and come to an agreement on reasonable actions to create as level a playing field as possible.

If there are religious holidays that fall during one of our class hours and days, and this holiday precludes you from attending class, please let me know by January 22nd. The university has published a fairly complete calendar of religious holidays. If you cannot attend, an alternative learning opportunity will be arranged.

The policy for absences caused by illness, personal or family emergencies, job interviews, varsity sports, etc. has been addressed under the section Absences.

A reminder that holidays such as Martin Luther King Day and the Spring break do not start days before designated times. Plan accordingly.

## RESOURCES NEEDED FOR THIS COURSE

Most of the resources necessary for this course are in your textbook, will be distributed as handouts, linked or identified in the Daily Assignment Descriptions, or exist collectively in the business core and elective classes taken over the past three or four years. However, there will be times where you must go beyond your present knowledge base and use the Internet, libraries, and other faculty as resources. What goes into a contract? How does one compute the Expected Value of Perfect Information? How do I compute the present value of a future stream of payments? What is meant by the book value of assets vs the market value under conditions of possible liquidation? What is the difference between a mussel and an oyster? What tools does a field sales manager have to gain compliance and buy in for territorial reallocations? These and other, will require learning on your own and from others.

**Technical Requirements**
You must have daily access to a computer that can reach the Internet, either of your own, a friend's, work or within the university. You must have an email account to facilitate communications and register on Blackboard under MKT 491 during the first ten days of the semester. Your computer skills must be adequate to effectively operate in programs such as PowerPoint, Excel and Word. Strong written and oral communication skills are expected of seniors at Miami University.

## E-SUGGESTION BOX
Please use this form for any suggestions that you wish to make. You are always welcome to see me before or after class, or during office hours in person with suggestions.
Name (optional): _____

Course & Section _____
I like....

I wish...

Other....

Go to the "G" public drive to get this form, as well as the Information Sheet and I Have Read Form.

## SYLLABUS AND CALENDAR CHANGES

I reserve the right to make alterations to this e-syllabus a any time if I believe that they will assist the class in more effectively or efficiently achieving the mission, vision, value or behavioral objectives of the course. All changes will be posted on the e-syllabus, announced in class, placed under Announcements or Flash Announcements of Blackboard, or all the above. It is your responsibility to be aware of these changes posted or announced in class within 48 hours of being posted. All changes will occur in the color orange.

## DAILY ASSIGNMENT DESCRIPTIONS (D.A.D.)

**Class #1**
Subject Matter: The E-Syllabus and B.A.R.S.
  - Distribution and electronic presentation of the e-syllabus
  - Introduction of the teacher and students
  - Taking of photographs for student information sheets
  - Thorough discussion of the e-syllabus and B.A.R.S.
  - Formulate BARS statements in small groups and submit

Behavioral Objectives:
  Why the extensive syllabus? If you are taking Marketing 491 as an elective, this e-syllabus will give you enough information to decide if you wish to stay or find an alternate course. You should have enough information to permit an "eyes open" enrollment in the course. It will require a lot of homework every week to learn and succeed.
  For more on the syllabus see "Justification for Detailed Syllabus" above.

Handouts:
  - Hard copy of e-syllabus up to daily assignments
  - Case Method Packet
  - Case Study *Quetzal Distributions, Inc.*
  - The Brand Called You article

Instructional Strategies:
  - Open electronic version of e-syllabus on system and the blackboard; handouts at the door; music on CD-ROM;

- Individuals at each of the bench tables will be asked to look over the e-syllabus and highlight areas where they may have questions. This should take about 25 minutes. Groups of three are then asked to record and later share their top two to five questions. While this is being done, I will take pictures of individual students;
- We will discuss each of these questions (25 minutes);
- Discuss B.A.R.S. and have ten groups prepare in writing one grade level; present some examples; have these turned in;
- Remind students to complete the two forms (Information sheet and Have-Read form) and to log into the Blackboard before next Thursday http://mymiami.muohio.edu/ ; also to carefully read the case method packet and try accessing this e-syllabus off my home page at www.sba.muohio.edu/GIFFORJB/Index.htm

**Class #2**
Subject Matter: Two Forms Due; The Case Study Method
- The Case Study Method
- B.A.R.S. Form returned and discussed
- Collect: Information Form & Have Read Form
- Exam Case Formats: Discuss

Behavioral Objectives:
- To understand and be able to apply the case study diagnostic process to solving problems in domestic and international business environments in your professional and personal lives;
- To be able to follow the guidelines for the preparation of case studies in terms of thought process and the mechanics of written format;
- To get you to start thinking about two partners for the first exam case;
- To convince you that this course will be time intensive and that the value you receive in this course will be in direct proportion to your input

Preparation Before Class:
- Review electronic version of the e-syllabus from my home page and write down any questions you have. Ask in class;
- Carefully review the Case Study Methods Packet and prepare any questions you would like to ask in class;

- Conduct a first reading of Quetzal Collections Inc.; make some preliminary notes concerning significant information contained within the case.
- Download and complete *Have Read...* and *Personal Information Forms*

Instructional Strategies:
- Collect *Have Read...* and *Personal Information* Sheets;
- Have students sign their photographs if ready; take pictures of late comers;
- Answer questions concerning any dimension of the e-syllabus
- Present each stage of the Model, along with examples from business situations;
- You are encouraged to ask questions at any time for clarification;
- PowerPoint or overheads, supported with commentary and discussion where appropriate will be used the entire class period

Bring To Class:
- Case Method Packet;
- *Have Read...* and *Personal Information Forms* (completed);
- Quetzal Collections, Inc. case;
- Basic factual case notes made on Quetzal;
- Questions you may have concerning the material in the Case Method Packet or E-Syllabus

Handouts:
- *Financial Aspects of Marketing Management*;
- *Financial Aspects of Marketing Management:* Textbook p. 589-600;
- *Marketing Metrics Problems  Day #1*;
- *Marketing Metrics Problems Day #2, plus Excel Income    Statements and Balance Sheets; Ratio Analysis; Other Marketing Metrics*
- *Number Crunching  A Refresher Course*
- *Ratios for Financial Statement Analysis, Methods of Valuation , and Company Analysis Sample*;
- *Appendix B· Financial Analysis*

**Class #3**

Subject Matter: Quetzel Collections, Inc. case, and *The Brand Called You* Discussion

Behavioral Objectives:
- To have you examine the definition and means to success in business;
To encourage you to act upon the concept of you being a "brand";
- To explore international dimensions of supply chain management, ethics, sustainable competitive differential advantage, niche marketing, economic supply and demand analysis, and importance of strategic planning;
To apply the Case Study Method to a relatively "simple" case
To start to get each of you to see both the forest and the trees at the same time and to think both within and outside the box. Read beyond and between the lines!

Preparation Before Class:
- Read, outline and think about the article "The Brand Called You";
Be familiar enough with the article that you could answer two out of three questions if we had a very short pop quiz;
- Read, outline and think about Quetzal Distributors, Inc. case; Prepare written notes concerning the S.W.O.T, Problem Statement, Alternatives, Decision Tree, Criteria, and some initial analysis.

Instructional Strategies:
- Discuss current event;
- Discuss article "The Brand Called You";
- In small groups, each group prepare one part of the Quetzal case on an overhead sheet;
- Discuss case collectively:
    - o    Overview intro
    - o    S.W.O.T.
    - o    PS
    - o    Alternatives & Decision Tree
    - o    Criteria
    - o    Analysis
    - o    Preliminary recommendation

Bring To Class:
- Article "The Brand Called You" and appropriate written notes;
- Quetzal Collections Inc. case and appropriate notes

Handouts:
- Case studies that are not in the book, through end of semester.

**Class #4**
Subject Matter: Marketing Metrics I - Problems 1-7

Behavioral Objectives:
- To remind you of some of the marketing, finance and accounting
- measures that relate directly to marketing decision-making;
- To introduce some of you to new concepts such as EVPI, sunk costs                   and                   cannibalization; To stimulate your general quantitative juices that have dried up over the past two years;
- To remind you that all you have learned in the business core courses and marketing major courses to date is essential in marketing problem solving and decision-making

Preparation Before Class:
- Read all the handouts on marketing metrics and financial management;
- Design an Excel matrix for the solution of each of the seven problems. These should include all data from the problems and use cell references to solve the problems. All the steps in the solution must be shown. Highlight the answers with a solid black border around each answer. Print each problem on a separate page centered horizontally and vertically. Be sure your names are one each page in the top left hand corner. Save your work, as these problems will come in handy for many of the cases you will complete    this    semester    and    in    business. You may work in sets of up to three persons, but each person must work on each problem! You will use the knowledge gained from these exercises all this semester and in your professional careers. It is essential that everyone in class can work out every part of every question!!! Make copies for each of you, but only hand in one set of the seven problems.

Instructional Strategies:
- We will spend the first 15 minutes in seven small groups preparing a   presentation to the class on one of the seven assigned problems; I will select the presenter from your group, so everyone must be an expert.
- As time permits, go over the other six problems to make sure you understand how to come up with the correct answers;
- Present the answers to the class as a whole on the board (50 minutes)

Bring To Class:
- Financial marketing management articles;
- Seven pages of printouts with you name (s) typed on the top of each page;
- Calculators

**Class #5**
Subject Matter: Marketing Metrics II

Behavioral Objectives:
- To increase your ability to interpret data from financial statements, resulting in an assessment of strengths and weaknesses of alternative marketing strategies;
- To familiarize you with ratio analysis of profitability, productivity, leverage and liquidity and their implications for marketers.

Preparation Before Class:
- You may work in groups of up to three on the following six bullet point assignments:
- Using the data provided on the "G" drive (download to your disk before starting); analyze Carling and Johnson & Quinn in terms of financial profitability, productivity, liquidity and leverage in 1996. Use the formulas and interpretation of outcomes provided in the handouts, MBA web site, and particularly the definitions provided on this website. Professionally present and interpret your findings. Always use cell references to compute these ratios.
- Carefully analyze both companies over the two-year period in terms of percentage changes and trends over this two-year period. Present your results as both tables and appropriate graphs. Be sure your graphs are full page and professionally created.

- How much should Johnson & Quinn offer to acquire three presses if installation and transportation per press costs $100,000? Total cost? Document and explain. What additional information is needed (hard and soft information)?
- IF Johnson & Quinn wants to purchase all of Carling, how much should the offer? Why? What is its value if purchased at 90%, 75%, 50% or 30% of book value? What additional information do you need to make a better assessment of the value of Carling to Johnson & Quinn? Legal options? Document all of the above.
- IF...IF...IF... Johnson & Quinn bought Carling for $2,500,000 on January 1, 1996 [ long-term loan from bank; payments = $500,000 per year plus interest of $81,000/yr ] produce and evaluate the combined income statements and balance sheets of J&Q on December 31, 1996. Assume no change in sales caused by the acquisition. Professionally interpret the results and present the revised Income Statement and Balance Sheet.
- In purely financial terms, verbally describe how much sales would have to increase (describe process) to achieve a net income (bt) of 2.8% for this combined entity. Start with the Income Statement created above.
- ALL SIX OF THE ABOVE SHOULD BE PREPARED ON THE COMPUTER USING THE SPREADSHEETS PROVIDED AS A STARTING POINT. YOU SHOULD BE READY TO TURN IN SIX SETS OF ANSWERS, EACH WITH YOUR NAMES AT THE TOP.

The above assignment is very difficult and will take the average very bright Miami University business student 6-7 hours. Plan accordingly. Save all your work, as the answers to all the above will be used when we do the case *Johnson & Quinn* later in the semester. At that time, we will add multiple marketing, strategy, positioning, niche, personnel, corporate culture, mission statements and HR dimensions to the analysis.

Instructional Strategies:
- Discuss your findings to each of the above six questions. The class will spend the first 20 minutes in small groups discussing one of the issues and preparing a presentation to the class as a whole. Everyone in that group should be ready to make the presentation. All materials will be collected at the end of the class for grading.

- Briefly introduce the next case, Henderson Electronics, and a few key things to be looking for as you analyze the case.

**Class #6**
Subject Matter: Henderson Electronics Corporation

Behavioral Objectives:
- To think in both macro and micro terms relative to channel systems (exclusive, selective, intensive);
- As a future marketing manager, to respond to a sales and profit directive through creative and objective revision of at least one critical marketing mix element;
- To audit an existing distribution channel system in terms of capacity to reach corporate objectives while simultaneously reaching a defined target market and the unique selling demands of a product category.

Preparation Before Class:
- S.W.O.T., PS, Alternatives, Criteria, Analysis and conclusions.
- Address each of the following questions:
- What is the marketing environment for Hendison Electronics Corporation?
- What are buyer requirements in purchasing home entertainment equipment?
- Should Hendison be using an exclusive, selective or intensive channel distribution system and why? TM? Channel capabilities?
- Analyze the pros and cons (against your criteria) of the following four alternatives:
  - Status Quo
  - Increase the number of dealerships: add 100 independent stores
  - Reduce dealerships from 475 to 150
  - Exclusive distribution with franchise-type arrangements: 77 to 100 dealers in 100 markets
- Back up each of the above with both strong qualitative and quantitative information and wisdom.
- Hints: Some key data to be objectively and creatively manipulated:
Retail/TV Outlets # = 4,289
Retail/TV Outlets Sales = $6,214,483,000
Retail/TV Outlets Average Sales per Outlet now = _____

Retail/TV Outlets Gross Margin Percentage of Retail = 27.5%
Retail/TV Outlets Wholesale Sales/Outlet = _____
Exclusive markets = 50
Non-Exclusive markets = 425
80% of sales in exclusive markets among 50 outlets
20% of sales in non-exclusive outlets [425]
10 salespeople [$80,000 each] make 24 calls/yr to each of 425
dealers over a 50 week period
1997 sales will increase 2.4% industry wide independent of action
Henderson must achieve a sales volume of $92,500,000 in 1997

Instructional Strategies:
We will draw two names from the jar who will present the SWOT, PS, ALT and Criteria. While they are writing these on the blackboard, the rest of the class will break up in small groups to answer the above questions and to consider the four alternatives. Two members from each group will be selected to present their groups findings. Once we have completed both of the above steps, the class will be asked to make a final recommendation to Richard Hawly, Vice President of Marketing.

Possible open-notes 120-second quiz!

Bring To Class:
- Well organized and legible handwritten notes and spreadsheets relating to all the above;
- Calculator

**Class #7**
Subject Matter: Drypers Corporation Case

Behavioral Objectives:
- To access the probability of achieving defined image and "pull" promotional objectives through expanded advertising in television;
- To practice selected advertising metrics such as objective-task approach versus competitive-parity budgeting;
- To reflect upon the correlation between "push" and "pull" promotional strategies and existing channel systems
- To learn *to compute market share point costs* and p*romotional BEP analysis.*

<u>Preparation Before Class</u>:
- Prepare a case analysis from S.W.O.T. through analysis and recommendations;
- Be ready to answer the following questions:
  * How would you characterize the US disposable diaper and training diaper market?
  * What is the competitive position of Dryper Corporation in the USA and international marketplaces?
  * Evaluate the existing and changing distribution channels for diapers.
  * What is Dryper's current grocery channel market share?
  * Should Dryper use a push or pull strategy?
  * Under what conditions does an advertising opportunity usually exist?
  * Relate the competitive-parity approach to Dryper's planned increase in advertising and existing budgets for the BIG TWO.
  *Assess the concept of a blitz media strategy to a more balanced approach for 1998.
  * What incremental Drypers brand sales will be needed to recoup the $10,000,000 dollar advertising expenditures on television? Probability of occurrence (judgment call)?

Note: A special group of six students will be invited to NOT answer the above questions, but will be provided with "insider information" available in January of 1999. Using this information, they will be asked to report to the class their evaluation of the success of the new campaign and make a specific recommendation for the continuation of the campaign in 1999. If you would like to volunteer to be part of this team, let the teacher know before the end of next class.

<u>Instructional Strategies</u>:
- We will discuss the case S.W.O.T., PS, Alternatives and criteria as a whole. Each of the above questions will then be answered (groups will be given 10 minutes to come to a consensus prior to their presentation).
- The class will be asked for their recommendations for Dryers Corporation senior marketing executives.
- A special group will then present an analysis of the outcomes for 1998 relative to defined criteria, and their specific recommendations for the total integrated marketing communications plan for 1999.

**Class #8**

Subject Matter: Croft Industries

Behavioral Objectives:
- To explore the relative power within the supply chain of a manufacturer who must sell a large proportion of their goods through distributors;
- Relevance of a regional price leader in an oligopoly environment;
- To consider the implications of demand and product substitution on pricing strategies;
- To learn to compute corporate and competitive break even points and to translate this information into strategic marketing pricing inputs;
- To look at micro and macro dimensions simultaneously.

Prepare before class:
- Read Croft Industries case and determine the strengths, weaknesses, opportunities, threats;
- Formulate a Problem Statement, Alternatives, Decision Tree, Criteria and Analysis at $17,$18, $19, $20 and $21 dollars per square.
- A professionally prepared graph of the sales trend in volume of squares for the region and Croft industries; bring 12 copies; you may work in groups of three.
- A professionally prepared table presenting the FC, VC, BEP(units), BEP ($$$s) for each of the alternatives determined; (Croft and Competitors, given probability of responses) you may work in groups of three

Instructional Strategies:
- Student names will be selected from the jar to present their S.W.O.T. and a general case overview; the class will be asked to assist in creating a complete SWOT;
- Five students will be asked to present their Problem Statements; these will be critiqued by the class and one amalgamated PS will be put together from these five.
- Three students will be asked to draw their decision trees; these will be refined by the class;
- In small groups, you will be asked to formulate criteria; these will then be shared.

- BEPs will be discussed; These will point toward a logical decision alternatives.

Bring To Class:
- Calculator

**Class #9**
Subject Matter: Strategic Marketing

Behavioral Objectives:
- To memorize and be able to apply the basic concepts involved in strategic planning in the twenty-first century;
- To understand the importance of systematic and continuous strategic planning in any profession, business or otherwise;
- To take careful notes so that you can apply the strategic planning process to your Strategic Business Unit next year in industry, education, the non-profit sector or government;
- To add the lexicon used in class to your problem solving vocabulary; phrases like "strategic window of opportunity" and others should become permanent parts of your professional vocabulary.

Preparation Before Class:
- Carefully review the large handout on strategic planning and identify areas of possible confusion;
- Think about how these concepts could be applied to a company or industry you may consider joining next year, or a company in which your parents or sisters and brothers are currently employed.

Instructional Strategies:
- This topic will be presented as a series of overheads presentation and represents the second lecture of the semester. There will probably be no more lectures during the semester.
- Please ask questions and offer examples whenever you are unclear or asked to by myself.

**Class #10**
Subejct Matter: Strategic Marketing Applied: Kimberly Wet Toilet Tissues

Behavioral Objectives:
- Strategic planning;
- New product introductions;
- Identifying corporate strengths, weaknesses, opportunities & threats;
- Introduction to marketing intelligence.
- Using pubic secondary information, identify and critically analyze Kimberly-Clark's goals (qualitative) and objectives (quantitative) for the corporation, and more specifically the Tissue division;
- Formulate a mission, value and vision statement based upon the interpretation of these goals and objectives for Kimberly – Clark, and more specifically their Tissue Division.   Based upon the mission, value, vision, goals and objectives, does the proposed new Cottenelle Fresh$^{TM}$ Rollwipes toilet paper represent a "good" product line extension?

Preparation Before Class:
- List at least  fifteen objectives of Kimberly–Clark   (to be typed and handed in at the end of class) 2-3 individuals per list ok;
- List at least 20 goals of Kimberly-Clark (to be typed and handed in at the end of class) 2-3 individuals per list ok;
- List of strengths, weaknesses, opportunities and threats (to be typed and handed in at the end of class) 2-3 individuals per list ok;
- Read "Toilet-Paper War Heats Up With New, Wet Roll" packet; Handout;
- Carefully read the following web sites and related links in order to be able to answer parts one, two and three. KC is having web problems, so not all the below links work consistently. Once on the home page, move around internally as much as possible. Investors and careers links from the home page are good doorways!
- You have received a one-page handout identifying both the key home          page          and          master          site          index. www.kimberlyclark.com
http://www.rollwipes.com/
www.kimberlyclark.com/index
http://www.careers.com/products.htm
http://www.kimberly-clark.com/news/
http://www.kimberly-clark.com/investorinfo/annual_report.asp
http://www.imberly-

clark.com/investorinfo/annualreport2000/kc_innovation.pdf
http://www.kcnonwovers.com/
www.newscom.com/cgi-bin/prnh/soo1o116/datuoo4-a
- Other electronic sources: See what you can find using the product and company name as search keys; try the top five search engines.
- Non-electronic media: Kimberly-Clark Annual Report 2001 is to be released at the end of the first week of February, and therefore will probably not be available to us. Try the 2000 Annual Report online.

Instructional Strategies:
- We will break up into eight groups to create master lists of goals, objectives and a single mission, value and vision statement per table. These will be written on overheads and presented to the rest of the class.
- We will collectively discuss the viability of  Cottenelle Fresh$^{TM}$ Wipes as a viable line extension and for fit with corporate goals and objectives (25 minutes)
- During the last five minutes, each student will be asked to write on a 5 x 8 card if the think Kimberly-Clark should proceed with this roll with a national roll out and the three most important facts that support your position. (5 MINUTES) - graded

Bring To Class:
- List at least 15 objectives of Kimberly–Clark (to be  typed and handed in at the end of class) - graded
- List at least 20 goals of Kimberly-Clark (to be typed and handed in at the end of class) – graded
- List of Strengths, Weaknesses, Opportunities and Threats (to be typed and handed in at the end of class)
- Other notes you have taken while viewing the websites

**Class #11**
Subject Matter: Johnson and Quinn I

Behavioral Objectives:
- To help you to learn how to assess the advisability of an acquisition, merger of a corporate entity... or its' assets;
- To have you analyze the value of selected assets under various conditions;

- To improve your ability to understand the various implications of combining two organizations;
- To provide to you a preliminary ability to assess the value of company;
- To further improve you qualitative and multi functional assessment skills.

Preparation Before Class:
- Carefully read the Johnson & Quinn case in the book;
- Review your notes from Marketing Metrics II
- Summarize the strengths and weaknesses of J&Q;
- Summarize the strengths and weaknesses of CPG;
- What problems are resolved by the acquisition of CPG by J&Q?
- What problems are created by the acquisition of CPG by P&Q?
  - Supply chain management
  - Quality control
  - Mission, goals and objectives
  - Competitive differential advantage
  - Markets and customers (present and desired)
  - Personnel, union, compensation and organizational issues
  - Operational and timing concerns
- What is the nature of the commercial printing industry and how should it influence Mr. Henkel's decision? (opportunities and threats)
- What are the relative negotiating power positions between the CEOs of both companies?
- What do you think about the $2,200,000 offer? What do they really get for their money?
- Be ready to discuss a Problem Statement, Decision Tree and Criteria for Johnson & Quinn.
- By the end of the class, we should collectively be ready to make specific recommendations to the CEO of J&Q concerning current action to be taken immediately and in the next 1-3 years.

Instructional Strategies:
- Individual groups will be asked to prepare answers to each of the above questions. These will be presented and discussed by the class as a whole.

**Class #12**
Subject Matter: Johnson and Quinn II

<u>Behavioral Objectives</u>:
- To summarize the qualitative evidence supporting or not supporting the continued attempt to acquire either the corporate entity or selected assets of PCG;
- To be able to compute the appropriate market value of CPG as an operating entity, out of bankruptcy, or fair market value of selected assets;
- To be able to compute the impact of an acquisition on the financial health and profitability of the acquiring company.

<u>Preparation Before Class</u>:
- Go to the "G" drive and download the series of spreadsheets stored under Johnson & Quinn;
- Complete all sections marketed in yellow;
- Create a series of printouts of your work; this should require a minimum of 4 - 6 printouts; add commentary on each page to interpret your findings; help J&Q make their decisions.

<u>Instructional Strategies</u>:
- We will discuss everyone's findings and the implications of these findings to the decision that needs to be made in the case.
- By the end of the class, we should collectively be ready to make specific recommendations to the CEO of J&Q concerning current action to be taken immediately and in the next 1-3 years.
- Tables with comments will be collected at the end of class.

**Class #13**
<u>Subject Matter</u>: P & G Always in Russia

<u>Behavioral Objectives</u>:
- To understand the S.W.O.T. of operating in a foreign country such as Russia, and to translate this understanding into operational and strategic decision-making skills.
- To explore the business environment of the largest country in the world (eleven time zones) that posses more natural resources overall than all of North America. In the next 10 years, you will probably be doing business in your job with Russian firms or American firms in Russia.
- To more fully appreciate the importance of cultural attributes as they impact products and services, pricing, promotion and supply chains.

Preparation Before Class:
- Read P&G Always in Russia case;
- Read the short handouts on P&G in Russia taken from the Internet;
- Make hand written notes concerning the following issues:
**A.**    What is the nature of television and direct mail promotion in Russia    in    the    late    1990s?
**B.**    What is the current pricing situation for P&G feminine protection products in Russia?  Be sure to look at the numbers and don't    rely    on    the    opinion    of    the    executives.
**C.**    How does the history and culture of Russia influence the purchase    decisions    of    women    in    Russia?
**D.**    How will political, economic and exchange rates conditions impact    the    success    of    *Always*    in    Russia?
**E.**    What security considerations must be accommodated for both P&G and their channel members to operate safely and profitably?
**F.**    What is the quality of the economic and marketing data available to P&G in making objective business decisions?  Explain.
**G.**    What is the difference between GDP and PPP?  Why is this important in most developing nations?
**H.**    Evaluate the age range of the target market selected by P&G and    relate    this    to    their    merchandising/marketing    mix.
**I.**    Discuss the dynamics of the competitive marketplace for feminine hygiene products in Russia.  What is the relevance of the existence of gray goods markets to this competitive marketplace?
**J.**    Discuss the realities of the political environment and doing business in Russia, short-run and long-run.  How does this relate to ethical    business    practices?
**K.**    One of the largest challenges to any company doing business in Russia is information systems and supply chains, both forward and backward.  How will this influence the probable success or failure of P&G in Russia?  Relate this discussion to manufacturing, wholesaling, conventional retailers, kiosks and pharmacies.

Instructional Strategies:
- We will watch a brief videotape on the new Russia at the time of our case.
- We will collectively discuss each of the above questions and relate the answers to the situation being faced by P&G.
- We will examine  collectively the case using the case method structure.

- May be a one question quiz based upon the questions posed above.

**Class #14**
Subject Matter: The Cottages Resort and Conference Center
EXAM #1 Case

Behavioral Objectives:
- To understand complex organizational and corporate structure and people priorities in decision-making;
- To conduct an in-depth analysis of:
    - Sustainable competitive differential advantages
    - Target marketing and positioning
    - People issues and priorities
    - Organizational structure
    - Industry analysis in area
    - Pricing issues
    - Promotional issues
    - Competitive issues
    - Facilities, location and physical issues
    - Financial issues such as BEP occupancy rate; BEP per sales person added, restaurant payback period or ROCI, and price change payoff matrix
    - SWOT
    - PS
    - Alternatives and decision tree
    - Criteria
    - Analysis of at least four alternatives
    - Decision, recommendation and implementation

Preparation Before Class:
- Carefully prepare answers to all the issues identified under the second behavioral objective above;
- Be ready to present the case in front of the class if name drawn from the jar.

Instructional Strategies:
- Two presenters will be selected from the jar and start working on the blackboard on the case;
- Groups of three will be asked to address two behavioral issues and prepare notes to share with the class;

- ▪ Discussion - everyone
- ▪ Conclusions and recommendations - everyone

Bring To Class:
- Calculator
- Typed Exam Case: Copy for each person plus one to turn in.

**Class #15**
Subject Matter: D. J. Joseph Company I

Behavioral Objectives:
- To introduce you to the operations of a heavy goods "gray" B2B industry rarely thought about, but vital to the industrial metals industry;
- To examine the necessary conditions for locating a new processing facility, given the nature of the marketplace;
- To help you understand the concept of isoprobability curves as they relate to supply and demand competition

Preparation Before Class:
- Be   ready   to   answer   the   following   questions:
   A. Discuss supply and demand side characteristics of the scrap metal industry 1) domestic and international and 2) in Henderson, Kentucky
   B. What are some of the major landfill and "Fluff" issues for DJJ in Henderson?
   C. What are the pros and cons of the site as it relates to 1). logistics 2) political considerations 3) competition and customer retention 4) timing 5) cannibalization  6) EPA.

Instructional Strategies:
- I will randomly ask individual students to answer each of the above questions and then invite others to add to the discussion;
- On day two, each pair of students will be asked to demonstrate their simulation and highlight the critical conditions under which DJJ will lose money if they open the Henderson site;
- The class as a whole will be asked to make a logical recommendation to DJJ concerning the opening of a processing plant at Henderson.

**Class #16**
Subject Matter: David J. Joseph Company II

Behavioral Objectives:
- To challenge you to design a simulation and demonstrate that simulation to the class. The simulation will be designed to determine the feasibility of a new site relative to <u>available tonnage of scrap</u>, <u>landfill costs to dump fluff</u>, and <u>selling price to industrial users</u>. This simulation must also compute: gross tons of scrap per month, cost of raw scrap, gross margin per ton, gross revenue per ton, operating expenses, current VC landfill per gross ton expenses, net profit before interest and taxes per month, net profit before interest and taxes per year, interest expenses per year per year, and net profit before taxes. You should be able to change price to industrial users, and have everything automatically adjust. This is a skill that will be needed in a broad variety of jobs in your future! By struggling on your own to create this simulation, you will learn more then if I just handed you the methodology. Use Excel.

Preparation Before Class:
- In groups of three, prepare a simulation matrix on a disk that allows you to enter the DJJ selling price of finished scrap per ton with the output of: cost of raw scrap, gross margin per ton, fixed operating expenses, net profit (bit)/month, net profit (bit)/year, net profit (bt)/month and net profit (bt) / year for all levels of gross tons and landfill costs from $5 to $12 dollars per ton. Find the critical levels of input dimensions that will determine the outcome of the site for DJJ. This may require you running a bunch of "What If... simulations (must be able to operate with only one number entered: the market price of scrap) runs will generate all 384 possible outcomes for all the measures above). You will be asked in class to demonstrate your excel simulation and explain your findings. In this simulation, it works correctly or doesn't work; there are no "sort of" models. We are talking about jobs and millions of dollars on the line!

Instructional Strategies:
- Each set of three students will be asked to demonstrate their simulation and highlight the critical conditions under which DJJ will lose money if they open the Henderson site;

- The class as a whole will be asked to make a logical recommendation to DJJ concerning the opening of a processing plant at Henderson.
- DISKS WILL BE COLLECTED, SO MAKE SURE YOUR NAMES ARE ON THE DISK AND THAT THE DISKS ARE BLANK EXCEPT FOR YOUR SIMULATION. PLACE NAMES ON THE DISK AND SPREADSHEET.

**Class #17**
Subject Matter: Shades of Black Case

Behavioral Objectives:
- To introduce you to decision-making in the small start-up business;
- To investigate alternative segmentation and channel strategies; given the human capital, physical facilities, and financial constraints typical of a small start up specialty business;
- To stretch your abilities to assess alternative actions, given limited input information; also criteria creation will be a challenge

Preparation Before Class:
- Carefully read the case and review the corrected financial statements on the "G" drive;
- Create well organized hand written notes on the S.W.O.T., PS, Alternatives, and Criteria;
- Use qualitative and qualitative analysis against your PS and criteria to determine both the desirability and FEASIBILITY of entering any one of the four or five alternatives.
- FYI: There were 3,456 black owned funeral homes in the United States and 480,00 deaths per year among African Americans in 1989;
- FYI: Almost all greeting cards are marked up 50% on retail (called keystone pricing).

Instructional Strategies:
- Two persons will be randomly selected to present the S.W.O.T., PS. Decision Tree and Criteria. During the time these are being recorded on the board, the rest of the class will work on evaluating the four or five possible alternatives using both hard and soft data/information;

- The class as a whole will assist your presenters through the entire case, resulting in a recommendation to Alex.

**Class #18**
Subject Matter: ALMA Case

Behavioral Objectives:
- To provide practice at assessing industry trends in the consumer leisure market;
- To review pricing strategies and considerations in consumer markets;
- To explore alternative pricing strategies and the impact of different supply channels on final consumer price points and CM;
- To create a second simulation to reinforce the learning experience gained from David J. Joseph.

Preparation Before Class:
- Create a series of five short simulations that will determine the contribution margin at six different logical price points under the conditions of 50,000 units or 100,000 units being sold. The five small simulations should be computed representing 100% retail distribution, 100% catalog distribution, 50% retail and 50% catalog, 25% retail and 75% catalog and 75% retail and 25% catalog. In the first condition (100% retail distribution at 6 different prices), compute: retail price, Units, BEP $$$s, Net CM if 50,000 units sold, and Net CM if 100,000 units are sold. Under condition two (100% catalog at 6 different prices), compute: retail price, retailer's cost, mfgr's FC, mfgr's VC, mfgr's CM, mfgr's BEP units, mfgr's BET $$$s, Net CM if sell 50,000 units, and Net CM if sell 100,000 units. For the next three conditions (50% - 50%, 25% - 75%, 75% - 25% at six prices), compute: average manufacturer's selling price, average mfgr's CM, mfgr's BEP units, mfgr's BEP $$$s, Net mfgr's CM at 50,000 units, and Net mfgr's CM at 100,000 units. Be prepared to justify logically why you selected the six price points (must be the same for all scenarios), given your criteria and the competitive marketplace. These simulations should fit on one page and be one Excel file. Be ready to turn in the printed version of your simulations.
- Create rough notes on the S.W.O.T., PS, Alternatives, and Criteria. These may be collected from selected rows in the class.

Instructional Strategies:
- We will spend the first 1/2 of class examining the SWOT, PS, Alt and Criteria for the case;
- We will spend the second half of the class exploring alternative pricing strategies, the product life cycle and pricing, and the alternative "What If..." pricing possibilities for Julie and Jim;
- Recommendations and supporting reasoning.

Bring To Class:
- Print outs of your pricing simulation
- Calculator
- Your hand drafted notes on S.W.O.T., PS, Alternatives, Criteria

**Class #19**
Subject Matter: Marketing Ethics: M-Ethics Game

There will be no homework for this class period before case Exam #2.
Be prepared to be open-minded and to have fun as we talk about developing your own set of personal and business ethics and play "Methics." Please bring a dime to class.

**Class #20**
Subject Matter: Apex Insurance Case I

Behavioral Objectives:
- To reinforce the importance of the concepts of comparative NPV, break-even point market share analysis and cash flow in service industries;
- To consider alternative channels of distribution in the service industry in a foreign setting, Canada;
- To reinforce the importance of the selection of the optimal target market (s) and the impact of this decision on the service package and promotion;
- To introduce the concept of cash flow as an important decision in selecting alternative service offerings.

Preparation Before Class:
- Be prepared to answer the follow questions:
    - A. What would be the characteristics of an ideal channel of distribution for the seed capital insurance policy?
    - B. Create a decision tree of the possible target markets.

    **C.** If the target beneficiaries are 0 to 2 years of age, and 85% of babies born in Canada are born to women in the ages 20 - 34 (Mean 26.9 yrs); and the birthrate in Canada is 1.09% per women in Canada, how many children are born every two years? What is the range of age of grandparents of these children in 1993? What is the range of age of great grandparents of these parents in 1993? How many of each of the above categories exist in Canada? (Use statistics for year 2000 attached to your case study - last page)

    **D.** What are the characteristics of an ideal educational endowment fund for parents? Grandparents? Great grandparents?

    **E.** Problem statement, Alternative decision tree, and Criteria for a GO decision?

    **F.** Strengths and weaknesses of Apex Life: Canada?

    **G.** Opportunities and threats facing Apex Life: Canada?

    **H.** What are the pros and cons of the R.E.S.P.?

    **I.** What are the pros and cons of the Universal Life?

    **J.** What are the pros and cons of the Seed Endowment?

    **K.** What are the pros and cons of using the M.G.A. channel for the S.E.

    **L.** What are the pros and cons of using Direct Mail for the S.E.?

• Complete the two Excel tables on the G Drive (may be collected)

    **A.** What media, mailing lists and co-operative partner (s) would you use to reach the primary target market you have selected?

    **B.** What media, mailing lists and co-operative partner (s) would you use to reach the secondary target market you have selected?

    **C.** Your recommendation and implementation strategy?

## Class #21
Subject Matter: Blair Water Purifier India Case

Behavioral Objectives:
• To continue our exploration of the unique challenges in marketing in the international markets such as India;

- To understand the impact of uncontrollable external environments on the distribution and pricing of a product originally designed for US markets:
- To analyze pricing and distribution alternatives in light of differential contribution margins and break even point market shares.

Prepare before class:

- In groups of one to three, complete the Blair Water Purifiers India word file outline by downloading and then filling in all the bullet points. If at all possible, please talk to a fellow student or faculty member to help with the differences between India and the United States. Print out our results to be collected at the end of class. You should also visit some of the sites on the Internet identified here, plus review the handout.

    http://www.kmike.com/country/indemog.htm
    http://www.kmike.com/country/in.htm#links

- Complete the four step spreadsheet provided on the "G" drive. Step five is optional and can be completed for extra credit. One cell in each of the answer tables has been completed to provide assistance. The output of this work will help you answer two of the questions on the word file outline.
- Write out as hand written notes the following information:
- Last Name A - J  = S.W.O.T.
- Last Name K - Z  = Problem Statement, Alternative, Decision Tree

Instructional Strategies:

- Over the class period we will discuss the SWOT, PS, Alternatives and Criteria, the bullet point questions and answers, the two web sites, the Excel spreadsheets, and the process of deciding to go international, plus alternative strategies for international expansion. Hopefully by the end of the class period we will be able to make objective recommendations to the management of Blair Water Purifiers concerning expansion into India (GO/NO GO) and if GO, how and at what price.
- Everyone will be asked to participate, and two individuals will be selected to facilitate this learning environment.

**Class #22**

Subject Matter: Chesterton Carpet Mills, Inc.

Behavioral Objectives:
- To explore a strategic and tactical point of conflict related to changes of patterns of doing business in a mature industry;
- To measure carefully the relative power positions and poker hands of various marketing institutions;
- To investigating multiple dimensions of TIMING, a critical success or failure component in most marketing decisions;
- To carefully assess the motivations, priorities, and risk tolerances of Suzanne Goldman, Assist to the President of CCM.

Preparation Before Class
- SWOT, PS, Alternatives, and criteria for Suzanne, the President and the Board of Directors;
- Evaluate the "what if..." implications of continuing their current channels with modifications or going direct to retailers. Significant obvious and not so obvious quantitative dimensions will need examination.
- Use in our computations carrying costs, holding costs, financing costs, inventory buildup, channel relations with retailers, pricing changes, and strategic pricing alternatives within the two alternatives.
- Be sure that all the "hard" data does not drive out the "soft" data.
- Hints:

  * I wonder what the comparative cost of adding our own warehouses and distribution system, including higher inventory levels, warehouses, sales managers, sales personnel, etc. would be relative to our current channel? Hmm...Interesting question.

  * I also wonder about the power position of our distributor(s) who have threatened to pull out. How strong is their poker hand? IF we decided on creating our own distribution system, I'm curious if their would be any timing or logistical or manufacturing complications?

Instructional Strategies:

- We will start by investigating as a total class the softer data that is relevant to Suzanne's decision making, plus the nature of the criteria involved in the decision by different parties;
- Secondly we will break the class in half and isolate all the financial savings and costs involved in each of the two alternatives. These will be compiled on the front blackboards.
- We will organize these so that there is a "bottom line" for each alternative.
- The class will be asked to combine all the soft data and hard data to make a final recommendations.
- We will probably only get as far as starting to explore all the financial considerations during the first class. You will be asked to record all of these and come to class on the 24th with an overhead of each alternative (groups of three) on a disk to be presented and modified by the class. I will also need a hard copy.

**Class #23**
Subject Matter: Scotia Aqua Farms Ltd. Case I

Behavioral Objectives:

- To introduce you to aqua-business, a huge business environment worldwide;
- To help you break down a business into its SBUs, and to examine the contributions of each SBU to the total business;
- To add to your knowledge base and understanding of the differences involved in aqua-business from other product businesses; for example, what is the book and market value of a mussel after 18 months growth?
- To require calculations and thinking in an international environment using non-USA measurements and currencies

Preparation Before Class:

- Read the case Scotia Aqua-Farms in the book pp. 141-156;
- Read the handouts *Farming Oysters* and *Who Grew that fish on your plate?;*
- Highlight in your mind and books/articles important facts about this industry in all three of the above sources so that you can answer a 35 question multiple choice quiz without using your notes;

- Prepare handwritten notes for the case of the S.W.O.T., PS, Alt, and Criteria. Save your analysis for the September 19th class;
- Be ready to answer the following questions:
    - **A.** What are the problems at Scotia Aqua Farms? What are their root causes?
    - **B.** How would you assess the individual attractiveness of the aqua-cultured:
      - oyster industry
      - mussel industry
      - trout industry

Instructional Strategies:
- Each group will be asked to prepare one of the above dimensions. For example, one group would be assigned the PS, Alt. or Decision tree; another the attractiveness of the trout business (domestic, international and for SAF)
- Groups will present their observations; the class will be asked to add to their observation, and to create a master list on our chalk boards
- Very good criteria (people and business) and alternative decision trees are extremely important in this case.
- There will be a 35-question quiz over the handout and case. It will be very specific and detailed. If will cover both the case details and the articles distributed in class. Closed book quiz.

**Class #24**
Subject Matter: Scotia Aqua Farms Ltd. Case II

Behavioral Objectives:
- To move from a general understanding of an industry and a specific firm within that industry, to qualitative and quantitative short-run and longer-run strategies and tactics for survival;
- To be able to break down the SBU's of a business and to assess their fit and financial feasibility;
- To continue to refine our skills at transforming data into meaningful information and then using that information to make specific tactical and strategic marketing action recommendations to management.

Preparation Before Class:
- Complete the eight tables saved on the "G" drive, add your names, and be ready to hand in at the end of class
- Create 2-3 professional charts that provides visual information that may have been missed by simply looking at these tables; These can reflect relationships beyond the 8 tables provided.
- Review your notes from the first day.

Instructional Strategies:
- In our individual groups, you will be asked to examine your "G" drive tables PRINTOUTS against those of your colleagues;
- We will collectively discuss each of the tables and its implications for Gordon
- The class will be asked to come to a consensus as to the best action (s) to be taken by Gordon Malcolm; what, how, where and when...

**Class #25**
Subject Matter: Hanover-Bates Case I

Behavioral Objectives:
- We will be looking at only two dimensions of this case. The first of these is the human dynamics. How should we handle the current situation to result in a win-win-win-win-win situation (Regional SM/Sprague/Carver/Other Sales Reps/Company)? What is the power structure of each group of stakeholders? How can we help everyone save face while achieving both corporate directed results and performance equal to or better than district seven?
- The second dimension is the analysis of all the data in the case, the conversion of that data into decision-making information, and the formulation of a very specific set of actions that will result in making all parties happy. The I. M. Yourboss memo is an excellent starting place for creating this information base, diagnostics, and decision strategy with payoffs. You'll need computations printed out to help with this second stage
- We will spend the entire week on these two initiatives!
- No spreadsheets are on the "G" drive
- Other than your final exam, this is your last case; maximize your learning by committing as much energy as possible, given your other academic commitments.

**Class #26**
Subject Matter: Hanover-Bates Case II
Continue discussion.

**Final Classes**
Bolter Turbine Negotiations I
Bolter Turbine Negotiations II
Bolter Turbine Negotiations III
Course Discussions and Surveys
- Review your notes from the first day.